Historical Problems:
Studies and Documents

Edited by
PROFESSOR G. R. ELTON
University of Cambridge

19
ORIGINS OF ENGLISH FEUDALISM

In the same series

ORIGINS OF ENGLISH FEUDALISM

R. Allen Brown
M.A., D.Phil., F.S.A.
Reader in History, King's College, London

LONDON: GEORGE ALLEN & UNWIN LTD
NEW YORK: BARNES AND NOBLE BOOKS
(a division of Harper & Row Publishers, Inc.)

British ISBN: 0 04 901020 4 hardback
British ISBN: 0 04 901021 2 paperback

Published in the USA 1973 by:
HARPER & ROW PUBLISHERS, INC.
BARNES & NOBLE IMPORT DIVISION

ISBN 06-490732-5 hardback only

Printed in Great Britain
in 10 point Plantin type
by Cox & Wyman Ltd
London, Fakenham and Reading

TO MURIEL

GENERAL INTRODUCTION

The reader and the teacher of history might be forgiven for thinking that there are now too many series of historical documents in existence, all claiming to offer light on particular problems and all able to fulfil their claims. At any rate, the general editor of yet another series feels obliged to explain why he is helping one more collection of such volumes into existence.

One purpose of this series is to put at the disposal of the student original materials illustrating historical problems, but this is no longer anything out of the way. A little less usual is the decision to admit every sort of historical question: there are no barriers of time or place or theme. However, what really distinguishes this enterprise is the fact that it combines generous collections of documents with introductory essays long enough to explore the theme widely and deeply. In the doctrine of educationalists, it is the original documents that should be given to the student; in the experience of teachers, documents thrown naked before the untrained mind turn from pearls to paste. The study of history cannot be confined either to the learning up of results without a consideration of the foundations, or to a review of those foundations without the assistance of the expert mind. The task of teaching involves explanation and instruction, and these volumes recognize this possibly unfashionable fact. Beyond that, they enable the writers to say new and important things about their subject matter: to write history of an exploratory kind, which is the only important historical writing there is.

As a result, each volume will be a historical monograph worth the attention which all such monographs deserve, and each volume will stand on its own. While the format of the series is uniform, the contents will vary according to need. Some problems require the reconsideration which makes the known enlighteningly new; others need the attention of original research; yet others will have to enter controversy because the prevailing notions on many historical questions are demonstrably wrong. The authors of this series are free to treat their subject in whatever manner it seems to them to require. They will present some of their evidence for inspection and help the learner to see how history is written, but they will themselves also write history.

G.R.E.

It is probably too much to hope that this slim volume might bring the glad cry of 'Game, Set and Match' in the too prolonged controversy over the origins of English feudalism. One fears it will not, if only because it is necessary to define your feudalism before arguing about it, and thus possible to alter the rules before beginning any new game or set in the interminable match. At least it may be felt that the volume belongs appropriately to a series devoted to Historical Problems, and that it is a good thing at last to have, gathered together in one place, and in translation, all those documents and pieces of evidence constantly cited and bandied about by the disputants, but seldom if ever seen, let alone read, by the willing but bewildered student. As for the Introduction, I have always felt and said that this subject was the *pons assinorum* among weekly essays: now my own turn has come (though I have taken more than a week in the attempt), and whether I have successfully crossed or not, I must leave to the judgement of my peers – and juniors.

I must thank, first and foremost, Professor Elton for taking on this volume and thus allowing me to get it off my chest, and next after that the many generations of undergraduates at King's College, London, who have severally sat through many trial runs in lectures and tutorials. I must also thank my College in another way, for giving me time eventually to prepare this publication, and my gratitude goes also to the publishers for producing it, and keeping down the price so far as in them lay. Many others have suffered in the course and cause of writing, including my dog in walks not taken and my mother in many lost weekends. None has suffered more than my poor wife, who has typed and checked and helped with the index and, in general, kept me sane. I could not be more grateful. Nevertheless the errors which will undoubtedly be discovered will also be found to be my own.

Thelnetham, Suffolk   R.A.B.
December, 1972

CONTENTS

PART 1: INTRODUCTION
The Origins of English Feudalism

I

Introductory

THIS volume is one of those which, in the words of the General Editor in his Foreword to the series, 'will have to enter controversy' – not so much, in this case of the origins of English feudalism, 'because the prevailing notions . . . are demonstrably wrong', as because the established, and correct, view, that feudalism in this country dates from the Norman Conquest as the direct result thereof, is nowadays once again attacked by would-be critics. Personally I regret both the controversy and the ensuing controversial nature of this volume, but at least let us hope that good manners no less than good sense may prevail, for as Maitland observed (in the first of innumerable references we shall make to him), 'It cannot but be . . . that this . . . work should be controversial though it need not be polemical.'[1]

There is such a thing as historical truth which, as it seems to me, is not always well served by wilful argument or the pushing of untried hypotheses, for while it may be urged that controversy is good for the student in that it forces him to think in order to decide which side he is on, my experience is that confusion is more likely to arise. While the weaker brethren will take refuge in the type of essay which sits solemnly upon the academic fence, proclaiming that 'while Professor A. states x, Dr B., on the other hand, says y', all students, whether at university or school, are usually unable to spend long periods pursuing a controversy to the original sources to test their interpretation for themselves, and thus are in the nature of things largely at the mercy of polemical writers. Certainly the responsible historian should think and ponder long before writing the kind of book or monograph designed to provoke debate, for we none of us live in an ivory tower nor write for fellow professionals only, and something once in print, however wrong, may take whole generations to eradicate by careful teaching.

Hence, then, this volume, to set the record straight, and to provide as much as possible of the evidence for doing so. Before we approach

---

[1] F. W. Maitland, *Domesday Book and Beyond*, 265. This and all subsequent references are to the paperback (Fontana, 1960) edition of a work first published in 1897.

closer to our proper subject, it is worth observing that controversy over the origins of English feudalism is set in the wider context of controversy over the Norman Conquest and the degree of its impact upon England. Few if any subjects have provoked more disagreement over a longer period than the Conquest, and few if any have been more bent by non-historical considerations,[2] participants tending not only to take sides[3] but also – worse and even nowadays – to commit the evident anachronism of seeing the pre-Conquest English as 'us' and the Normans as 'them'. In our own time, while it may still be taken further, up to the ultimate question of whether the Norman Conquest is to be seen as a Good Thing or a Bad Thing, the more moderate academic debate is between continuity and discontinuity. Roughly speaking, all English-speaking historians are agreed upon the peculiar excellence of England, especially in matters governmental, after the Conquest, and the question is, who, English or Normans, contributed what and the most to this outcome. Within this context, moreover, there has been a marked swing of historical opinion in the course of this present twentieth century, measured appropriately enough by the life and work of the late Sir Frank Stenton, whose *William the Conqueror*, first published in 1908, was wholly different, in its critical attitude to Anglo-Saxon achievement, from the sympathetic appreciation of his *Anglo-Saxon England*, first published in 1943. The trend has since continued far beyond the magisterial survey and analysis of Stenton's latter work, until a recent writer can proclaim, touching the Norman Conquest, that 'for half a century or so from 1066 the English way of life was not sensibly altered. The Normans had very little to teach, even in the art of war [*sic*],[4] and they had very much to learn. They were barbarians who were becoming conscious of their insufficiency.'[5] As a consequence of this sort of thing, I wrote in another place that 'upon English historians in the twentieth century the influence of the Anglo-Saxons has increased, is increasing, and ought to be diminished'.[6] Yet, as there is little new under the sun, so there is little new in attitudes to the Conquest, and thus G. K. Chesterton was provoked to remark concerning the continuity-men of his own day, '[A

[2] See D. C. Douglas, *The Norman Conquest and British Historians* (David Murray Lecture for 1946; Glasgow, 1946); Christopher Hill, 'The Norman Yoke' in his *Puritanism and Revolution* (London, 1958).

[3] A former tutor of mine, the late Idris Deane Jones, once observed that 'history is a mere rattling of dead men's bones unless we breathe into the ghosts and memories of the past the life of our personal sympathies and judgements' (*The English Revolution*, London, 1931, 13).

[4] The only authority cited in support of this quite extraordinary remark is Richard Glover, 'English Warfare in 1066', *English Historical Review*, lxvii, 1952, for which see below, p. 36.

[5] H. G. Richardson and G. O. Sayles, *The Governance of Medieval England* (Edinburgh, 1963), 27.

[6] *The Normans and the Norman Conquest* (London, 1969), 6.

man] may end by maintaining that the Norman Conquest was a Saxon Conquest'.[7] Albeit of great importance in its own right, the question of the origins of English feudalism fits into this wider context, for if Old English society was already feudal, or proto-feudal, when the Normans came, then here is continuity, and if feudalism in England is a Norman importation, then here is discontinuity and also, surely, one of the most wide-ranging changes which the Conquest wrought.

So now to settle to our proper question of the origins of English feudalism, while certainly first noting that for Selden and other seventeenth-century antiquaries still living with or close to feudal tenures there was no doubt of their Norman introduction, we need otherwise go no further back in terms of historiography than John Horace Round and Frederic William Maitland, for it is upon their work that both the rival schools of modern thought are based. The conventional and established view, that feudalism is a Norman innovation, springs from Stenton out of Round. Round's great paper, 'The Introduction of Knight-Service into England',[8] first published in the *English Historical Review* in 1891-2 and subsequently as a chapter of his *Feudal England* (1895), took the cataclysmic view, of sudden and fundamental change, and argued it to the hilt with the ruthless and sometimes arrogant clarity characteristic of that great but maddening historian. 'I am anxious to make absolutely clear the point that between the accepted view [i.e. of continuity, in 1895] and the view which I advance, no compromise is possible. The two are radically opposed.'[9] Round in his seminal essay dealt only with one central and fundamental point, *viz.* the introduction of knight-service into England, which is also the imposition of the quotas and the introduction of the fief. He was wise to do so, for such precision is essential if the presence or absence of feudalism is to be argued, and it is not to be shrugged off by Maitland's smiling references to the 'feudalist of the straiter sort'.[10] In this controversy we must all be feudalists of the straiter sort in order to know what it is that we are arguing about. Sir Frank Stenton, in his Ford Lectures for 1929, having paid due tribute to Round, advanced the argument further into other and scarcely less important aspects of feudalism, and, *à propos* of continuity in the shape of the theory of pre-Conquest English feudalism, delivered a verdict which also serves as a definition of feudalism, though couched in negative terms: 'It is turning a useful term into a mere abstraction to apply the adjective "feudal" to a society which had never adopted the private fortress nor developed the art of fighting on horseback, which had no real conception of the specialization of service, and allowed

[7] *Orthodoxy* (London and New York, 1909), 126.
[8] Discussed below, pp. 62-6.
[9] *Feudal England*, 261.
[10] *Domesday Book and Beyond*, 198.

innumerable landowners of position to go with their land to whatever lords they would.'[11] We may subsequently wish to qualify Round's insistence upon the *constabularia* of ten knights as the unit of the feudal host upon which the new Norman quotas were based,[12] and Stenton's insistence upon specialialization of service,[13] but it is from the work of these two historians that the present-day conventional view is derived.

Meanwhile the contrary view is derived from Maitland, and the modern would-be argument for pre-Conquest English feudalism, in spite of the recent publication of the Red Book of Worcester and the alleged new evidence it provides,[14] is largely Maitland's argument restated, at times more loudly and certainly without the subtlety and percipience of his unrivalled scholarship. Maitland had waited for Round's *Feudal England* to appear before publishing his *Domesday Book and Beyond* in 1897,[15] but this was in order that he might have the benefit of Round's 'Domesday studies' in the former work: the 'Introduction of Knight-Service into England' he must have already known at least from its first appearance in the *English Historical Review* in 1891–2, and it did not prevent him from setting down in his new book the most persuasive argument that there is for feudalism in England before 1066.[16] No further advance has yet been made, nor, one supposes, can be. It is perhaps as well to emphasize in this present volume chiefly intended for the student, who is young, that the latest and most recent views, expressed in criticism of Stenton and of Round, are in reality *passés* and *déjà vus*, and have no novelty about them: hence the splendidly crushing remark of Professor R. R. Darlington – 'the arguments are the old ones which we had thought dead, and resurrection does not make them any more convincing.'[17]

[11] F. M. Stenton, *The First Century of English Feudalism* (Oxford, 1932), 215.
[12] Below, p. 64.
[13] Below, p. 71.
[14] Below, pp. 66–71.
[15] *Domesday Book and Beyond*, 5.
[16] *Ibid.* 194–201, 354–75.
[17] R. R. Darlington, *The Norman Conquest* (Creighton Lecture, London, 1963), 24.

II

Frankish Feudalism

WHAT, then, was this feudalism whose presence or absence in pre-Conquest England is almost the whole of our problem? – for no one can seriously doubt that England was feudal after 1066,[1] nor that Normandy was feudal not only after 1066 but also before.[2] It is here that we most need clarity of thought and precision of definition or analysis, but very seldom find them. It is not that the words feudal and feudalism are themselves incapable of at least as much meaningfulness and accuracy as any other general portmanteau terms used to describe types of society, e.g. socialist, capitalist, democracy and the like, as that our words, feudal and feudalism, are in danger of becoming, or have already been made, peculiarly imprecise by their usage. This may be in part because both are later words, unknown to contemporaries, coined by historians afterwards to describe a state of affairs already past or passing. Thus we do not meet 'feudal' in the English language until 1639 in the works of Spelman, the 'feudal system' first appears in 1776 in the works of Adam Smith, and we have to wait for 'feudalism', curiously enough, until 1839.[3] In any case, setting aside the arrogant ignorance of those politicians, publicists, journalists and television pundits for whom 'feudal' is merely a more insulting epithet than 'medieval',[4] even historians differ

[1] Below, p. 83.
[2] Below, p. 84.
[3] See *New English Dictionary*.
[4] Disapproval is even found among historians who should know better. On this point Maitland is worth quoting at some length: 'There are indeed historians who have not yet abandoned the habit of speaking of feudalism as though it were a disease of the body politic. Now the word "feudalism" is and always will be an inexact term, and, no doubt, at various times and places there emerge phenomena which may . . . be called feudal and which come of evil and make for evil. But if we use the term, and often we do, in a very wide sense, if we describe several centuries as feudal, then feudalism will appear to us as a natural and even a necessary state in our history. . . . If we use the term in this wide sense, then (the barbarian conquests being given us as an unalterable fact) feudalism means civilization . . .'. For the whole passage see *Domesday Book and Beyond*, 267–8.

in their usage of the word and may be divided roughly into the two categories of those who use it in the broad sense and those who use it in the narrow, i.e. Maitland's 'feudalists of the straiter sort'. In the former category, Marc Bloch is surely the greatest, for in his book, *Feudal Society*,[5] he touched upon almost every feature – including, for example, the difficulties of transport,[6] or the age at which men died[7] – of that period which for more particular reasons we, and he, call feudal. In this respect, therefore, Bloch's *Feudal Society* is to be compared and contrasted with F. L. Ganshof's *Feudalism*,[8] with its close analysis of the origins, development and fusion of those elements of commendation – fealty, homage, investiture – which form the personal bond between lord and man basic to feudal society.[9]

An analysis and survey of feudal society so wide-ranging as, in effect, to use the epithet 'feudal' as synonymous with 'medieval' is all very well for the historian of a place and period where feudalism is not in doubt; but if it is in doubt, as with pre-Conquest England, we obviously must be more precise. It is very much to the point that Bloch's own definition of feudalism includes elements which are not, in fact, peculiar to it: 'A subject peasantry; widespread use of the service tenement (i.e. the fief) instead of a salary, which was out of the question; the supremacy of a class of specialized warriors; ties of obedience and protection which bind man to man and, within the warrior class, assume the distinctive form called vassalage; fragmentation of authority – leading inevitably to disorder; and, in the midst of all this, the survival of other forms of association, family and State . . . – such then seem to be the fundamental features of European feudalism.'[10] Now all these things may have been 'fundamental features' of feudal society, but many of them are not essentially feudal, i.e. are not confined to the feudal period. Obviously those 'other forms of association, family and State', are not, for if they were both the Romans and ourselves would partake of feudalism. Nor is 'the fragmentation of authority' (which did not in the feudal period, *pace* Bloch, lead 'inevitably to disorder' – the association of feudalism and disorder being the most pernicious of modern heresies, albeit appearing, as here, in the highest places). Nor – perhaps less obviously at first sight since the feature is so heavily stressed at least in the popular view of feudal society, but a point of crucial importance to our understanding and to this debate – nor is 'a subject peasantry' peculiar to feudalism, nor of the essence of it, since it exists before and after the

[5] English edition, trans. L. A. Manyon, London, 1961.
[6] Pp. 61–2.
[7] Pp. 72–3.
[8] English edition, trans. P. Grierson, London, 1952.
[9] Below, p. 28. For Ganshof's own discussion and definition of the wider and narrower meanings and usages of the word 'feudalism', see *ibid*. xv–xvi.
[10] *Feudal Society*, 446. Cf. p. xiv.

feudal period and in societies in no sense feudal. Bloch himself, indeed, was very well aware that a subject peasantry and the manor existed as a matter of historical fact outside feudalism and, further, that the ties of dependence which bound the peasants to their lords and to the soil were of a type and development different from those superior ties of vassalage which bound their lords to each other.[11] It follows, therefore, at once for our purposes, that the facts that manorialization was proceeding apace in many parts of pre-Conquest England, and that the Anglo-Saxon free peasant, the ceorl, was losing his freedom in practice if not in law, are largely irrelevant to the issue of the origins of English feudalism.[12] Also by thus paring away inessentials, namely those things which are not unique to feudal society, we begin to approach a true conclusion, namely that feudalism, strictly defined and thus properly understood, is an upper-class affair. This glittering superstructure may have rested upon the broad backs of the peasantry but was by no means unique in so doing, and the peasantry is no more essential to the definition of feudal society than the bourgeoisie who were also present in increasing numbers at the time, but who also, even more than the peasantry, are very much still with us in the unfeudal present.

What we still want from Bloch's definition of feudalism is that which still remains of it, that is the fief, the supremacy of a class of specialized warriors, namely knights, and the ties which bound that class together, namely vassalage. This remainder brings us very close to the definition of feudalism essayed by one of its latest historians, Professor C. W. Hollister, himself, like Round and Ganshof, and as is necessary, a 'feudalist of the straiter sort' – in his case concentrating upon the central and crucial issue of the organization of military service.[13] For Hollister, feudalism is an organization of society 'based on the holding of a fief, usually a unit of land, in return for a stipulated honourable service, normally military, with a relationship of homage and fealty existing between the grantee and the grantor'. It is true that from such a strict and academic definition all the glamour, and therefore something of reality, has been stripped away – the chivalry, the eagles and the trumpets, the captains and the kings. We can bring them back again

---

[11] *Feudal Society*, 241–8.
[12] Cf. below, pp. 44–5.
[13] The following definition will be found, curiously enough as a footnote, to p. 11 of C. W. Hollister's *Military Organization of Norman England* (Oxford, 1965). This volume forms one of a pair with his slightly earlier *Anglo-Saxon Military Institutions* (Oxford, 1962). In the later volume especially, Hollister is on the side of the angels in seeing feudalism in England as a Norman importation, albeit affected here by pre-existing English customs and institutions. This approach is entirely reasonable, though in every instance the author may be thought in practice to exaggerate the degree of pre-Conquest English influence, and thus of 'continuity'.

anon, but meanwhile in the bare bones of this definition (more especially if we drop the cautious qualifications 'usually' and 'normally', as for purposes of strict and close analysis we can), we find certain fundamentals once more as we did in Bloch and Stenton: the ties of fealty and homage which make vassalage (to which we must often obviously add investiture with the fief), the fief itself, and military service.

It is a fault that none of the definitions of feudalism so far cited specifically refer to knights, for we need Stenton's 'art of fighting on horseback' and Bloch's 'class of specialized warriors', and the latter in the feudal period are the knights – in their native France *chevaliers* – mounted warriors *par excellence*, specialized and heavily armed cavalrymen, at once a military and a social élite, whose elaborate equipment and social elevation continue to distinguish them from any other cavalrymen the age may subsequently produce, whether their own esquires, for example, serving the long apprenticeship of knighthood, or the inferior horsed 'sergeants' of the twelfth century and later. The knight is of the very essence of feudalism, more fundamental than the fief, which, after all, was devised for his support.[14] Indeed, while certain of the elements which will develop and combine to form feudalism can be traced back to a remoter past, its true origin is to be found in the adoption of heavy cavalry by the Franks in the eighth century – a dramatic instance of the effects of warfare upon society, and therefore of the importance of military history.[15] Before this time in the west, whether among the Romans or their Germanic successors, cavalry had played at best only a secondary role in war,[16] and the Franks especially had traditionally fought on foot (hence their characteristic weapon, the *francisca* or battle-axe): by about the middle of the eighth century, for reasons still

[14] Below, p. 29.

[15] H. Brunner's classic thesis that the origins of feudalism are essentially military with social repercussions remains unbroken though not unchallenged. See *Deutsche Rechtegeschichte* (Leipzig, 1887–92; 2nd edition with additions, Leipzig, 1906–28). Useful reviews of the literature on the origins of continental feudalism and its development will be found in Carl Stephenson, 'The Origin and Significance of Feudalism', *American Historical Review*, xlvi (1940-1) and Lynn White, *Medieval Technology and Social Change* (Oxford, 1962), Chapter I.

[16] One needs to know more of these matters, but the development of heavy cavalry is certainly dependent upon the use and exploitation of the horseshoe, the saddle and the stirrup as technological aids to good horsemanship and the realization of the horse's potential. All were essential to the heavy cavalry of the Middle Ages, not least the stirrup without which the favourite and characteristic shock tactic of the charge would have been impossible. Thus Lynn White (see previous note) argues for the adoption of heavy cavalry by the Franks in the mid-eighth century as the result of the introduction of the stirrup to the west at that period. See also Bloch, p. 153; F. Lot, *L'art militaire et les armées au moyen age en Europe et dans la proche Orient* (Paris, 1946), i. 19–20; cf. *Past and Present, 24 (1963).

uncertain,[17] they had made heavy cavalry the dominant arm, the point of effective change being generally taken as 755 when King Pepin altered the date of the annual assembly of Frankish magnates and the host from March to May, i.e. the season of the first forage.[18] From this basic, military fact a new social, ruling class was to arise, built up by the Carolingian kings and emperors and establishing itself in the collapse of the Carolingian state in the ninth century.

The association of knighthood and gentility, ultimately even nobility,[19] begins early, and inevitably so – and is not to be postponed, as it is by some modern historians, to the later twelfth century and the later Middle Ages.[20] No doubt the earlier Germanic warrior-retainer,

[17] The traditional reason, as from Brunner, is the need for cavalry revealed by the invading, mounted armies of the Arabs in the eighth century. For the stirrup, see previous note. It has also been suggested that what was new among the Franks in the eighth century was not the appreciation of the potential of cavalry but the ability to support this expensive weapon through the invention of the benefice or fief (R. H. C. Davis, *A History of Medieval Europe*, London, 1957, 125).

[18] Lot, i. 92–3; Bloch, 153; Lynn White, 3–4.

[19] Bloch, 291.

[20] Thus Stenton, *Anglo-Saxon England*, 628; 'The ordinary knight of the eleventh century was a person of small means and insignificant condition . . .'; *First Century of English Feudalism*, p. 142; 'although knighthood in the eleventh century implied military proficiency, it carried no social distinction . . .'. In the second instance Stenton cited first in evidence the rarity of the use of the word *miles* as a 'mark of distinction' in charters of the twelfth century. The point is important as indicating the status of the knight, and it is therefore important to note that the word *miles* is in fact so used, for example, in Norman charters from the tenth and early eleventh centuries (e.g. M. Fauroux, *Recueil des actes des ducs de Normandie, 911–1066, Mémoires de la Société des Antiquaires de Normandie*, xxxvi, Caen, 1961, p. 60. Cf. e.g. p. 70, No. 2, p. 89, No. 13, p. 433, No. 225), as it is also in one of the earliest English charters of enfeoffment to survive, that in favour of Roger de Lacy, *miles*, in 1085 (V. H. Galbraith, *English Historical Review*, xliv. 372, and below, p. 90, Doc. 50). Cf. also R. Allen Brown, *The Normans and the Norman Conquest*, 46–7. The most recent and elaborate exercise upon the theme of the lack of social distinction of early knights is that of Miss S. Harvey, 'The Knight and Knight's Fee in England', *Past and Present*, No. 49, November 1970, which came to my attention after most of this present book had been written. This seems to me to rest upon two misconceptions: first that all instances of the word *miles* in Domesday Book can be assumed to mean knight (at that time and place – see below) and used for statistical purposes; second, and more profoundly disturbing, the concept of a dichotomy between what are variously called 'professional', 'active' and 'fighting' knights, as opposed to upper-class, gentlemanly and aristocratic knights who are apparently above the sordid business of actually fighting. In the ethos of that society, so remote from the standards and tastes of our own, about which we all have the temerity to write albeit with little understanding (to make riding compulsory for all history students might help a little), one would rather have supposed that the higher your social standing the harder you would be expected to fight. Miss Harvey also cites the evidence of charters and does not find the style of *miles*/knight until the thirteenth century (p. 42).

to the degree that he was full time, also needed to be released from, and thus raised above, the sordid necessity of tilling the soil, and waxed in wealth and prestige in measure as he was successful. But the advent of the warhorse greatly augmented these factors and the otherness of the warrior who bestrode it. No longer did the best people fight in the same manner as their social inferiors, and to fight on horseback is in itself expensive and became increasingly so as standards rose.[21] You needed a horse, which soon became no ordinary horse but one specially bred and trained. You needed more than one such horse, as you nowadays need more than one pony to play polo. You needed servants or attendants to care for your horses and furbish your increasingly elaborate, and costly, gear. And especially you needed time, and freedom from all other occupations, to devote to training and exercises, begun at an early age, and to provide that service which, as we shall see,[22] you owed to your lord as his vassal. 'You can make a horseman of a lad at puberty; later than that never' – thus an early Carolingian proverb, to be echoed by a later German poet, 'He who has stayed at school till the age of twelve and never ridden a horse, is only fit to be a priest'.[23] Hence, in eleventh-century Normandy, for example, the long apprenticeship of the young men, *tirones*, esquires, before the arms of knighthood were bestowed upon them,[24] or the full-time, residential service in the household of a lord, glimpsed in the pages of Ordericus Vitalis or Gilbert Crispin's 'Life of Herluin'.[25] Hence the professionalism, for these men were as professional as the age could make them. Hence the near total dedication to war and feats of arms, mirrored in the secular epics and *chansons de gestes* composed to be read for their entertainment.[26] Hence the cult of knighthood, and hence the cult of chivalry,[27] whereby we bring back again into the analysis of feudalism the glamour of the eagles and the

[21] Bloch (p. 152) notes that in the Ripuarian Law a horse cost six times as much as a cow, as did the *broigne*, later to be superceded by the more expensive hauberk. He also cites the case, in 761, of a small landowner of Swabia who sold his ancestral fields, together with a slave, to buy a horse and sword. See also K. Leyser, *English Historical Review*, lxxxiii, 1968, p. 11 (in an article, entitled 'Henry I and the beginning of the Saxon Empire', which traces the somewhat belated emergence in tenth-century Saxony of a small military élite of heavily armed and mounted warriors, *milites*, on the West Frankish model, to meet the menace of the Magyar light horse).

[22] Below, p. 29.

[23] Quoted by Bloch, 152, 293–4.

[24] Cf. Brown, *The Normans and the Norman Conquest*, 47 and n. 152.

[25] *Ibid.*, 48. See Ordericus Vitalis, *Historia Ecclesiastica* ed. M. Chibnall (Oxford, 1969), ii. 30, 54, 132; J. Armitage Robinson, *Gilbert Crispin* (Cambridge, 1911), 87–90; Doc. 20. Cf. Ordericus on the Earl of Chester in Doc. 32.

[26] Cf. Bloch, 293, quoting Bertrand de Born. Doc. 41.

[27] As Denholm Young remarked (*Studies in Medieval History presented to F. M. Powicke*, Oxford, 1948, p. 240) you cannot, by definition, be chivalrous without a horse.

trumpets, the captains and the kings. Thus knighthood early and inevitably became an upper-class affair, and so remained.

Of course at no time were all knights great men, but from an early date all great men were knights,[28] which ensured the social distinction of the institution even though each generation will produce its quota of landless knights and even (comparatively) poor knights, as it produces younger sons, and young men on the make, and failures. Meanwhile this military élite, worth more now in war (and here is the reverse of the coin) than the less well armed and less skilled foot-soldier who is the common-man and peasant, becomes, in this society essentially military in its ethos, a social élite also. There is much history in words, and by the late tenth and early eleventh centuries in France and Normandy the Latin word *miles*, meaning in classical times and for centuries thereafter, simply any 'soldier', had come to mean 'knight' – the knight who, in his own eyes and those of his peers at least, monopolized and exemplified the military virtues.[29] The knights were thus launched on their long career, at one and the same time both an officer class and a ruling class, and the *force de frappe* of medieval armies, their charge the ultimate offensive weapon. Amongst outside observers of Latin Christendom, Anna Comnena, daughter of the Eastern Emperor, at the time of the First Crusade, was much impressed, and declared that the mailed Frankish knight would penetrate the walls of Babylon.[30] Another, the Arab Emir Ousâna, observed with admirable sociological percipience that among the Franks 'all preeminence belongs to the horsemen. They are in truth the only men who count.'[31] To our own day cavalry regiments have an exclusive social distinction, and the superiority of the man on the horse (for which there is no modern equivalent, not even a Rolls Royce) derives directly from feudal society.

It was inevitable also that the new dominant class of knights coming to the fore in the eighth and ninth centuries should become a landed aristocracy since almost all wealth, prestige and status was then, and for

[28] Thus in pre-Conquest Normandy the young Duke William the Bastard was knighted in his adolescence, his biographer, William of Poitiers, characteristically assuring us that the news alarmed all France (William of Poitiers, *Histoire de Guillaume le Conquérant*, ed. R. Foreville, Paris, 1962, p. 12). The knighting on a later occasion, in 1087, of his son Henry by the Conqueror is described in some detail by Ordericus Vitalis (ed. A. Le Prévost, iii. 267). At this date in Norman and Anglo-Norman society the conferment of knighthood was a ceremony of note. Cf. Brown, *Normans*, 47. See also p. 42 below.

[29] Bloch, 162; K. J. Hollyman, *Le développement du vocabulaire féodal en France pendant le haut moyen age* (Paris, 1957), 129–34; Hollister, *Military Organization of Norman England*, 115–16; Lynn White, *Medieval Technology*, 30 and n. 5.

[30] *The Alexiad of Anna Comnena*, ed. and trans, E. R. A. Sewter (Harmondsworth, 1969), 416. Doc. 40.

[31] Cited by Bloch, 291.

centuries after, derived from land. We thus begin to approach the knight's fee or fief, an institution so fundamental to any definition of feudalism that from its Latin form, *feudum*, the very words feudal and feudalism are derived. But in fact we can only approach this fundamental by way of another, namely vassalage, for in the development of feudal society in Carolingian Gaul vassalage, like the knight, precedes the fief, which only subsequently brings a property element into what is at first the purely personal relationship of lord and vassal. Of all the elements of feudalism, vassalage has the longest pedigree, since its origins can be traced back to the private armies of late Roman magnates and/or to the *comitatus* or war-band of the German tribes, described by Tacitus in his *Germania* as early as the first century AD.[32] This, the group of armed retainers about a war-leader, so prominent a feature of early Germanic and therefore early Frankish society, was unlikely to decline in the circumstances of the endemic civil wars of Merovingian Gaul. The Carolingians in their turn made much use of 'vassals' both to attain power and to govern their over-mighty state, and it is at this time, significantly, that the words *vassus* and *vassalus* came into general use for the sworn military retainer.[33] Then, with the collapse of the Carolingian state and of central authority in ninth- and tenth-century Gaul, under the reiterated blows of Viking and Muslim and Magyar, when 'the only effective authority was the one on the spot',[34] society painfully reformed itself on the basis of vassalage, of local lordship. It became, in short, feudal society. 'The king has now nothing save his title and crown . . . he is not capable of defending either his bishops or the rest of his subjects against the dangers that threaten them. Therefore we see them all betaking themselves with joined hands to serve the great. In this way they secure peace' – thus a German prelate, quoted by Bloch,[35] describing the kingdom of Burgundy about the year 1016. It is now, as a matter of historical fact, that the new knightly ruling class establishes itself, that the new princely families, comital families and baronial families, who are to make the future history of Latin Christendom and more, emerge from the ashes of the old world to hammer out the new.[36] During this time also the status of the warrior-retainer, now the vassal,

[32] Tacitus, *Germania*, c. 13–14; Latin extracts in W. Stubbs, *Select Charters*, 9th. edition, 62–3; translation in *Tacitus on Britain and Germany*, H. Mattingly (Penguin Classics, 1948), 111–13; Doc. 1. Cf. Stephenson, *American Historical Review*, xlvi. 798–806.

[33] Ganshof, *Feudalism*, 20–21; Bloch, 155–6.

[34] Bloch, 65.

[35] P. 160.

[36] Cf. Bloch, 284. R. W. Southern has a splendid sentence on the early counts of Anjou as typical of the new princely families – 'War made them conspicuous, grants of land established their position, marriage consolidated it, and the acquisition of ancient titles of honour cloaked their usurpations' (*The Making of the Middle Ages*, London, 1953, p. 82).

steadily rises, not least because, as we have seen, he has become a specialist mounted warrior, a knight, and, as the tactics and equipment of mounted warfare increase in sophistication, is ever more sharply distinguished from the ordinary free peasant, now of less and less military value and declining towards servitude. From Merovingian times there had been an act of commendation whereby one man placed himself under the protection of another more powerful. Now in the ninth and tenth centuries, marking the growing gulf between knight and peasant, upper and lower class, and (as they will become) free and unfree, there develops a special and elevated type of commendation out of the undifferentiated original, restricted to the high level of lords and vassals whose relationship it creates, and distinct from lower forms of commendation, also developing, whereby a peasant is bound by servile bonds to his master, the lord of the manor.[37] The former is that full feudal or vassalic commendation which, since it both creates and symbolizes the principal bond of secular society, at the upper levels where it matters most, is so fundamental that feudalism cannot be said to exist without it. It consisted of three parts. The first and the most important was the act of homage, when by the *immixtio manuum*, by placing one's joined hands (in what is still the attitude of prayer, i.e. rendering homage to God) between the hands of the lord, one became his man, his vassal. This solemn, visual and symbolic act of subordination might be accompanied by a kiss to confirm it and to stress the element of equal friendship (one did not kiss one's serf). Second came the oath of fealty which hallows the basic act of homage with religious sanctions. Thirdly and finally, but not necessarily since the vassalage already created can stand without it, there was investiture, whereby the lord symbolically invested the vassal with his fief (Docs. 2, 3, 39).

At this point, then, we reach the fief, our third fundamental of feudalism. The relationship created by vassalic commendation is bilateral, a voluntary association between two free men, once created irrevocable save for a serious default of obligation on either side, otherwise ending only with the death of either party. The principal obligation of the vassal is service, especially military service, which from an early date is knight-service. The principal obligation of the lord is the maintenance of his vassal. In the west where economic, more specifically commercial and urban, decline had so far been continuous and cumulative from the third century AD, salary and wages in money were out of the question. While therefore maintenance could be provided in kind in the lord's household (and the household vassal and the landless knight are more lasting features of feudal society than is often allowed as one generation succeeds another), nevertheless the normal method by the ninth century had become a grant of land to live on and from, first

[37] Ganshof, *Feudalism*, 25; Bloch, 160–2.

called the 'benefice (*beneficium*) and later the 'fee' or 'fief' (*feudum, feodum*).[38] The fief in its classical feudal form is a parcel of land bestowed upon the vassal, to be held by him of his lord as a tenant, reverting to the lord on the death of the vassal,[39] and in return for which the vassal owes his lord that service which is due, especially military service, specifically knight service.[40] Hence the knight's fee of post-Conquest England: hence the *fief de haubert* of eleventh-century Normandy – from the *haubert* or hauberk, the long mail coat of the knight as shown, for example, on the Bayeux Tapestry.[41]

So far we have thus identified three fundamentals of feudalism – the knight, vassalic commendation, and the fief. It seems necessary lastly to add a fourth, namely the castle, duly listed as 'the private fortress' in Sir Frank Stenton's definition of feudalism cited above, but too often ignored by English historians.[42] It is therefore worth emphasizing, though there is nothing original about the proposition, that the castle belongs uniquely to feudal society as the creation and manifestation thereof (which fact points again to the upper-class reality of feudalism – 'The rich man in his castle. The poor man at his gate'). Nor is this surprising since fortification, like all warfare on the one hand and all architecture on the other, directly reflects the society responsible for it and is an integral part of the social complex. As a matter of historical fact the castle finds its origins in the ninth and tenth centuries in the dissolving world of Carolingian Frankia which saw also the crucial development of those other fundamentals of feudalism with which we have been dealing, just as it also declines as a viable institution with the decline of feudalism itself. Further, if one enquires what it is that distinguishes the castle from other types of fortification both earlier and later, and wherein lies its uniqueness and its feudality, the answer lies in its definition; for the castle is a fortified residence, uniquely combining the dual role, and moreover it is the private, as opposed to public, and the residential fortress of a lord, who may or may not be the King or Prince. It is true that the private nature of the castle may need to be qualified by the over-riding rights of public authority, lingering in the first feudal age and rapidly reviving in the second,[43] but yet also the reality of this

[38] The word 'fief' first appears in the late ninth century. See Ganshof, 96; Bloch, 163–7.

[39] Below, p. 91.

[40] For other services see below, p. 91.

[41] The best edition of many is that by F. M. Stenton and others (*The Bayeux Tapestry*, 2nd. edn., London, 1965). Doc. 75.

[42] For Stenton see p. 19 above. See also E. S. Armitage, *Early Norman Castles of the British Isles* (London, 1912). The French, of course, are fully aware of *le château féodal* as part of their feudal heritage: see e.g. Bloch, 300, 400; Guilhiermoz, *Essai sur l'origine de la noblesse en France*, 143–65.

[43] See the unpublished (London, Ph.D.) thesis by C. H. Coulson.

private as opposed to public nature is re-emphasized if we think again of the castle's dual role, not just a fortress but also the residence of a lord. Certainly the post-feudal and so-called 'modern' era in Western Europe holds no equivalent, its fortresses being purely military and also national, while the whole difference in concept (and social context) between the feudal castle and the larger communal fortifications – Iron Age forts, Roman camps, Anglo-Saxon burghs – of older and other societies (surviving into our period often enough as fortified towns) can still be seen vividly on the ground by means of an aerial photograph of an Old Sarum or a Portchester.[44] Certainly also, in the minds of contemporaries the castle was closely associated with that type of military and militant lordship which we call feudal and of which it was both symbol and substance. The castle stood for lordship in men's eyes. 'You shall have the lordship, in castle and in tower' – thus the envoys of the Young King in England in 1173, seeking to win over the King of Scots to their enterprise by offering him the northern counties.[45] The very word *donjon* (dungeon) applied by contemporaries to the principal tower which was the principal strength of many castles (and which usually contained the principal residential apartments for the lord) was derived from the Latin *dominium*, meaning lordship. And to this day in France, where, with some significance, the word *château* is retained for the large country house of a gentleman, there, if you want to find the real thing as opposed to some modern mansion, you are well advised to ask not just for *le château* but for *le vieux château féodal*.

Maitland wrote that 'of all the phenomena of feudalism none seems more essential than seignorial justice',[46] yet so far we have not considered it. It is, of course, true that in feudal society a lord will have an automatic (and entirely logical) jurisdiction over his vassals at least in pleas relating to land held of him and the services relating thereto, and it is also true, as we shall subsequently need to note,[47] that the honorial court where such justice is dispensed becomes a prominent feature of England after the Norman Conquest, though we do not hear of it before. Nevertheless, Maitland in thus pushing seigneurial justice into the centre of the stage (compared with it, he could see military tenure as merely 'a superficial matter') wrote as the lawyer rather than the historian. Ganshof will now allow jurisdiction as any part of the original nexus of vassalage,[48] and certainly in the origins and development of private jurisdiction, whether in Frankia or England, there are other

---

[44] Doc. 78.
[45] Jordan Fantosme, *Chronique de la Guerre entre les Anglois et les Ecossois*, in *Chronicles . . . of Stephen, Henry II and Richard I*, ed. R. Howlett, vol. iii (Rolls Series, London, 1886), 227.
[46] *Domesday Book and Beyond*, 307.
[47] Below, p. 93.
[48] *Feudalism*, 31.

factors to be considered than the purely feudal, as, for example, public or popular and local justice, the franchise or delegation of royal jurisdiction, and that low-level jurisdiction of a semi-agricultural kind which the lord of a manor or estate is bound to acquire over his subject peasantry. Seigneurial jurisdiction may be, with others, a feature of feudal society, but we shall do better to exclude it from the basic fundamentals where it does not belong and without which feudalism cannot be said to exist.

Finally it may seem desirable to end this section with some definition of that feudalism which it has analysed, if only because we shall assuredly be taken to task by critics, and (more important) by students, if we do not. Any such definition must clearly incorporate, and indeed be based upon, those four fundamentals, each a unique feature, which have been discussed. Feudal society, then, over and above all other features more or less characteristic, and which may vary, more or less, according to time and place, is a society dominated by a secular ruling class of knights, at one and the same time forming both a social and a military élite, bound to each other, in a hierarchy culminating in the prince, by vassalic commendation, and holding their lands (or most of them, or that part of them which gives the holders their particular status) by knight service as fiefs. Such a society is also distinguished by that peculiar type (amongst others) of fortification which we, and they, call the castle, combining the two roles of personal residence and fortress both private and public. To such a society, but to no other, the adjective feudal may properly and meaningfully be applied.

III

Pre-Conquest England

WE have now thus analysed and isolated the four fundamentals of feudalism. We turn next to pre-Conquest England. In an examination of late Old English society on the eve of the Norman Conquest, we must evidently find all four of them before that society can properly be called feudal, whereas if, in fact, we find none of them, the argument for pre-Conquest English feudalism obviously cannot stand. Before we begin, however, there are one or two introductory considerations touching the nature of the evidence and our interpretation of it. First, it is, of course, true that it is always difficult to prove a negative, in this case the absence of feudalism, and historians frequently and rightly warn against the dangers of negative evidence. Yet to establish a negative fact we are bound to adduce negative evidence, and that evidence may in this case be thought in itself conclusive.[1] Further, the argument against pre-Conquest English feudalism is not only negative: it can be shown that Old English society was something other, and positive, in its own right, and for good reason, and therefore was not feudal. Second, it is also of course true that we could wish for more evidence than we have (namely the literary evidence of chronicles and histories, the documentary evidence of charters, writs, laws and the like, and archaeological evidence), and true also that very often a cloud of unknowing seems to descend upon just those features of Anglo-Saxon or Anglo-Scandinavian history of which we need to know most. Yet, again, although the evidence for this period of history, for England as for elsewhere, may seem sparse by the standards of later periods, and especially so for secular affairs since the Church had a near monopoly of literacy, there is nevertheless sufficient to show a clear and overall pattern. And in such circumstances, it may be urged, they do wrong who seize upon some unrelated fact, even if, at first, it does not seem to fit, and raise upon it, in isolation from the rest, some broad hypothesis or sweeping theory out of keeping with that pattern and the likelihood of things. Third and last, though the continuing or revived controversy about the origin of English

---

[1] Thus Mrs Armitage in seeking to establish the absence of castles in pre-Conquest England (*Early Norman Castles*, 11). Cf. p. 73 below.

feudalism has naturally produced much recent work, not all of this has been in the most appropriate directions. Thus there is as yet no equivalent for England to Ganshof's close study of Continental commendation, nor has there been in this country any comprehensive linguistic study of feudal terminology and its development.[2] Perhaps no two undertakings are more needful at this present time. Meanwhile the absence of the latter has led to loose talk, even in the highest places, historians of pre-Conquest England using without justification such strictly feudal terms as homage, knights or even castles, thus consciously or unconsciously prejudicing the argument though proving nothing.[3] Again it is at bottom misguided that so much of the attention of English-speaking historians has been centred upon the single question of the presence or absence of the fee in pre-Conquest England. One can appreciate the train of thought, for assuredly the fee or fief is a fundamental of feudalism; but the fundamental, archetypal fief which we must have in order to be feudal is the knight's fee, the *feudum militis*, the *fief de haubert*, and to pursue this in splendid isolation from any serious concern for the presence or absence of the knight is to put the cart before the horse and lose touch with reality, for in the real world of the early Middle Ages the knight is of necessity anterior to the fee.[4]

1. *Absence of knights*

We must therefore begin our survey of Old English society with a search for knights, though, to anticipate, we shall not find them. Anglo-Saxon society, of course, in common with all Germanic societies, had known its *comitatus*, the warrior band, and the armed retainers of kings and other magnates, the *gesiths* of the earliest sources. The Danish wars of Alfred's time and after had seen the *gesiths* replaced by new men, the thegns, similarly beginning as retainers and warriors, and becoming in their turn a landed aristocracy long before the Norman Conquest.[5] It is doubtful, indeed, how far the thegns still formed an effective military élite by 1066,[6] and in this role their part had to a large extent been taken over by the housecarls of Cnut's Danish conquest and settlement –

---

[2] Cf. for France, K. J. Hollyman, *Le développement du vocabulaire féodal en France pendant le haut moyen âge*. Stenton however, both makes use of terminological evidence and offers many valuable contributions to its study in his *First Century of English Feudalism*.

[3] Thus, for example, pre-Conquest knights appear in Maitland's *Domesday Book and Beyond* at 357, 361, 363 (together with 'what in substance are knights' fees' at 199); homage appears in Stenton's *First Century of English Feudalism* at 130, and in his *Anglo-Saxon England* at 510, 556; the 'burh-gate' is translated as the 'castle-gate' in *English Historical Documents*, i. 432.

[4] Cf. p. 24 above, and p. 45 below.

[5] Cf. H. R. Loyn, 'Gesiths and thegns from the seventh to the tenth century', *English Historical Review*, lxx (1955).

[6] Cf. Stenton, *First Century*, 119.

a fact to remind us again that Anglo-Scandinavian rather than 'Anglo-Saxon' is the appropriate epithet for pre-Conquest England. Certainly the housecarls of the King and earls formed the most professional element of pre-Conquest 'English' armies, and it is for this reason, no doubt, that they have usually been singled out by the exponents of pre-Conquest English feudalism as the best candidates for knighthood.[7] Yet no less likely candidates could be found. Not only did the housecarls, like the English thegns and peasants, fight on foot, but they excelled at it, and in so far as they were a professional military élite so were they also the most formidable infantrymen in western Europe, their famous and characteristic arm, the dreaded two-handed battle-axe, being of necessity an infantry weapon, impossible to wield in the saddle. 'Weapons dictate tactics'[8] indeed, and the axe had long since been abandoned by the Normans, those former Norsemen but now inveterate horsemen, more Frankish than the Franks.[9] In short and, as it were, by definition, the Anglo-Scandinavian housecarls were not knights: nor, by the same token, were the Old English thegns – nor, obviously, such of the peasantry as took part in battles and campaigns. The absence of cavalry in pre-Conquest English armies is a telling point against the notion of pre-Conquest English feudalism, one almost sufficient to bear the whole weight of the argument by itself, for without cavalry there can have been no knights, and without knights there can have been no feudalism.

The Norman and Anglo-Norman knight may sometimes have dismounted in action as occasion demanded (as in sieges, for example, he was bound to do), but he was first and foremost a cavalryman:[10] this was his *raison d'être*, and the point need no further be laboured.[11] While, therefore, it is perfectly possible to have cavalry without knights, as all Western nations did in the nineteenth century, it is inconceivable that

[7] Thus Hollister, *Anglo-Saxon Military Institutions*, 138; Richard Glover, 'English Warfare in 1066', *English Historical Review*, lxvii. 16.

[8] Glover, *English Historical Review*, lxvii. 4.

[9] It is misleading of Glover in this respect to cite the Bayeux Tapestry as evidence that the battle-axe 'is no English monopoly' (4), for the only time it appears in other than English hands is ceremonially in the hands of Count Guy of Ponthieu, who is not a Norman (*Bayeux Tapestry*, ed. Stenton, Pl. 12).

[10] Far too much is customarily made by English-speaking historians of the known occasions of the dismounting of Anglo-Norman knights for battle in the twelfth century, at Tinchebrai, Brémule, Bourg Théroulde, Lincoln and the Standard. Latest in the field is Hollister, *Military Organization of Norman England*, 127–8 and elsewhere (see Index). One simply cannot sweep aside the cult of the horse in feudal Europe by pointing to exceptions, nor dismiss the efficacy of the charge by citing occasions when it was not used. The cavalryman can fight on foot: the infantryman cannot fight on horseback. See Lot, *L'art militaire*, 315–19.

[11] See above, p. 24.

any society in the mid-eleventh century could have knights but yet no cavalry. The straight military question, therefore, of whether pre-Conquest English armies used cavalry or not, whether any part of them fought on horseback or not, is directly relevant to, is almost tantamount to, the bigger question of the nature of that society of which those armies were a part. It is thus not surprising that in recent years when the argument for pre-Conquest English feudalism has been revived, an argument for pre-Conquest English cavalry should also have been put forward, notably by Mr Richard Glover.[12] Nor, given the almost total neglect of medieval military history by English-speaking historians, is it surprising that it should have been uncritically accepted in some quarters.[13] Yet the argument will not stand up to any detailed examination. In the first place, that the English, unlike the Franks in Gaul, should not have adopted cavalry, is not of itself a problem demanding explanation: the problem is, rather, to explain why the Franks changed to cavalry, not why the English did not.[14] History teaches (or should) that military organization and tactics are an integral part of society, not easily changed, and certainly the Anglo-Saxons had been under no compulsion to change their time-honoured tactics of infantry warfare since their only external foe had been the Vikings who likewise fought on foot, as did the native Celtic races beyond the borders of the English kingdoms. The military changes or developments brought about by the prolonged Danish wars, which extended in all from before Alfred's day to the final conquest by Cnut in 1016, were the adoption of fortifications known as burghs or boroughs,[15] and a notable revival of naval warfare. Both these developments were compelled by the opposing tactics of the Danes, but there was no such motivation for the adoption of cavalry. There is abundant evidence to show that the battles of these wars were infantry engagements. The *Encomium Emmae Reginae*, for example, describes Swein Forkbeard's army landing in England in 1013 and preparing to fight on foot, makes it clear that Cnut's army for his invasion of 1015 was an infantry force and specifically calls Ashingdon in 1016 a severe infantry battle.[16] In the detailed description of the Battle of Maldon, in Essex in 991,[17] both sides fought on foot, and the tactics of the ealdorman Brihtnoth on the English side were almost exactly those of Harold at Hastings some half-century later. 'Then he bade each warrior leave his horse, drive it afar and go forth on foot, and trust to his hands and to his good intent.' Brihtnoth himself rode up and down the

---

[12] 'English Warfare in 1066', *English Historical Review*, lxvii, already cited.
[13] Thus Richardson and Sayles, *Governance of Medieval England*, 27.
[14] Above, p. 24.
[15] Below, p. 74.
[16] Ed. A. Campbell, Camden Third Series, lxxii (London, 1948), 13, 21, 27.
[17] 'The Song of Maldon', translated in *English Historical Documents*, i, ed. D. Whitelock, 293. Doc. 18.

ranks to counsel and array his men, then he 'alighted among the people where it pleased him best, where he knew his bodyguard to be most loyal'. As the Danes, 'the wolves of slaughter', advanced across the river, he ordered his forces to form a shield-wall, the defence which so long resisted the Normans in October 1066 – 'He bade them form the war-hedge with their shields, and hold their ranks stoutly against the foe'.

Of course English and Danes alike, ealdormen and earls, thegns and housecarls, and any others who were able, rode on the march, but this, and only this, is meant by references to 'horsed armies' in pre-Conquest English chronicles.[18] References, indeed, to the military use of horses are fairly frequent in the sources, and come early as well as late. Thus in Alfred's time, long before any existing argument for English cavalry, we are told by Florence of Worcester (a later writer using earlier sources) that in 876 the Danes broke the treaty which had been made with them and 'killed all the horses which the king had'.[19] The same writer provides a particularly revealing glimpse of what is involved, and of the sort of use made of horses in these campaigns, in his report of an action by Danes from England against the Franks in Gaul – 'the battle finished, the heathen, having found horses, became horsemen'.[20] Horses could be used not only on the march but also in both flight and pursuit, which is clearly what is happening in a well-known passage of the Anglo-Saxon Chronicle for 1016, which cannot possibly be made to bear the inter-pretation sometimes put upon it of the employment of cavalry on the field of battle – 'And the Danish army fled before him [king Edmund] with their horses into Sheppey. The king killed as many of them as he could overtake.'[21] In the old-world society of pre-Conquest England, if you were prosperous you rode to battle: if you were lucky, you rode away; but for the engagement itself you dismounted and fought it out on foot, in the time-honoured manner. There is one other piece of evidence, from the very eve of the Norman Conquest, and which may be thought to echo the authentic ring of truth. Both Florence of Worcester and the Anglo-Saxon Chronicle tell us of a reverse of the English in 1055 at the hands of the Welsh because the Norman Earl Ralph of Hereford, King Edward's nephew, made his native levies 'fight on horses contrary to their custom'.[22] Here surely is a touch of military reality, as one of

[18] See J. H. Clapham, 'The Horsing of the Danes', *English Historical Review*, xxv (1910). For references to *equestres exercitus* and the like, see e.g. Florence of Worcester, *Chronicon ex Chronicis*, ed. B. Thorpe (London, 1848–9), i. 212, 221, 222, 225.

[19] Ibid. i. 93.

[20] i, 97–8.

[21] *Anglo-Saxon Chronicle*, ed. D. Whitelock and others (London, 1961), 96. Doc. 4. Cf. Glover, who, however, has the grace to hedge a little by suggesting the passage is evidence for 'some sort of fighting on horseback' (p. 9).

[22] Florence, i, 213; *Anglo-Saxon Chronicle*, ed. Whitelock, 130. Docs. 8, 17.

Edward's 'Norman favourites', already established in Herefordshire before the Conquest, sought to wage the type of warfare to which he was accustomed and bring his English forces up to date, with the result, inevitable without long training, of chaos and disaster. It has been argued by Glover that the incident is only of local, and not of general, significance, because the Welsh border is remote and unsuitable for cavalry.[23] In fact it is evident from both accounts that the action took place at or near Hereford, which looks like perfectly good cavalry country today, and in any case after 1066 the Norman knights were to ride triumphantly through the Marches and deep into Wales.

Against all this there is only one item of allegedly positive evidence for the use of cavalry by pre-Conquest English armies – and that is false. It is the account in Snorre Sturlason of the battle of Stamford Bridge, fought in September 1066 before Hastings, by Harold of England against the invading force of Harold Hardrada of Norway.[24] It is a Norse saga source, part thus of a suspect class of evidence, written down in the thirteenth century and therefore far away in both time and place from the events it purports to describe. To depend upon it unless it is confirmed by closer and contemporary evidence is to break the accepted canons of historical scholarship – still more so of it conflicts with all such other evidence.[25] The degree of dependence which can in fact be placed upon it is sufficiently shown by its reference to armoured horses,[26] used in the thirteenth century but scarcely in the mid-eleventh. There are other demonstrable errors also, but they are not all, for it is impossible to read Snorre Sturlason's account of Stamford Bridge without the nightmare feeling that one is reading not of that battle but of Hastings, three weeks later, but with the roles and parts reversed, with Harold's English cavalry charging up the hill as the Normans were to do at Battle, and Harold Hardrada's Norwegians resisting on foot at the top of it as Harold of England's army was then to do.[27]

That in the event Harold's Anglo-Scandinavian force at Hastings in October 1066 dismounted before the battle and fought it out on foot to the end (when some fled on horseback),[28] is a fact admitting of no possible doubt, being vouched for by the unanimous testimony of the ample contemporary evidence which makes Hastings amongst the most fully

[23] Glover, 8.
[24] *The Heimskringla or the Saga of the Norse Kings*, ed. R. B. Anderson (London, 1889), iv. 41ff. See also the paperback, *King Harold's Saga*, ed. Magnus Magnusson and Hermann Palsson (Harmondsworth, 1966), 144ff. Doc. 19.
[25] Cf. therefore Glover, 5–9.
[26] Ed. Anderson, 44; ed. Magnusson, 149. Doc. 19.
[27] A point duly noticed by both E. A. Freeman, *The Norman Conquest* (Oxford, 1867–79), iii. 720, and C. Oman, *A History of the Art of War in the Middle Ages* (2nd. edn., London, 1924), i. 150–1.
[28] *Bayeux Tapestry*, ed. Stenton, Fig. 73.

recorded engagements of the earlier Middle Ages.[29] We even have, from the Norman side, echoing down the ages, what must be one of the earliest notes of the cavalryman's contempt for the foot soldier incapable of getting off his flat feet.[30] This incontrovertible fact, it can be seen, fits exactly the overall pattern, military and civil, so far outlined above. It needs no further or special explanation, and is certainly not to be explained away by the special pleading attempted by Glover, viz. that faced with the necessity of a defensive action Harold dismounted his cavalry, that is his housecarls, to stiffen the ranks of the rest.[31] Such an hypothesis is not merely incapable of proof but runs clean contrary to all the evidence we have of pre-Conquest English tactics. Moreover, at this point we can bring forward yet other evidence from the Tapestry itself, which in military matters (as in others) is under some compulsion to be true since it was commissioned for display among contemporaries, including those who took part in the great adventure of 1066.[32] Thus though the Tapestry contains a superb portrayal of Harold both armed and mounted before the action begins,[33] in the battle scenes he and all his followers, high and low, not only are on foot, but also none wear spurs, some, including some of the best-armed earls and housecarls, still have the old round shield of infantrymen,[34] and many, including Harold himself, wield the great two-handed battle-axe which that day wrought such havoc.[35] The scene of the death of Harold, in which the King, on foot with an axe, is cut down by a mounted Norman with a sword, may at the last remind us of William of Malmesbury's remark, that the point of Duke William's taking Earl Harold with him on the expedition into Brittany in 1064 was that 'he [Harold] might perceive how far preferable was the Norman sword to the English battleaxe'.[36]

Nor are the differences between the two sides at Hastings to be reduced and minimized by the attempted playing down and derogation

---

[29] The most recent account of the battle, with a full citation of the sources (listed in n. 115 to p. 164), will be found in Brown, *Normans*, 163–74. The best contemporary account is that of William of Poitiers (Doc. 27).

[30] Thus the contemporary Guy of Amiens' *Carmen de Hastingae Proelio*, in *Scriptores Rerum Gestarum Willelmi Conquestoris*, ed. J. A. Giles (London, 1845), 38; and thus Wace, *Roman de Rou*, ed. H. Andresen (Heilbronn, 1877–9), ii. 372–3.

[31] Glover, 17.

[32] If the recent argument be accepted that the inspiration of the Tapestry is more that of the secular epic than of religion (in so far as the distinction can be made) then this point is all the stronger. See C. R. Dodwell, 'The Bayeux Tapestry and the French Secular Epic,' *Burlington Magazine*, civ. 1966.

[33] Ed. Stenton, Fig. 58.

[34] See Figs. 64–5 (the death of Earls Leofwine and Gyrth), 70, 71, 72.

[35] See Figs. 62–3, 64, 65, 67, 70, 71–2.

[36] *Bayeux Tapestry*, ed. Stenton, Fig. 72; William of Malmesbury, *Gesta Regum*, ed. W. Stubbs (Rolls Series, London, 1889), ii. 293.

of the specialized horsemanship of the Norman knights, and by Glover's unwise talk of 'infantile Norman mounted tactics'.[37] The shock tactic of the disciplined charge of heavy cavalry was in process of development at this time,[38] with the Normans in the van, not, of course, as the single and invariable role of knights but as the ultimate weapon. Certainly, while one or two references elsewhere suggest that the technique might still be employed upon occasion,[39] very few if any of the Norman knights at Hastings on the Tapestry are acting as 'mounted javelineers' armed with 'javelins' and 'throwing spears'.[40] The majority are wielding their lances overarm or underarm in the ancient and classical manner of horsemen against foot-soldiers. On this issue one may add that all those lances of the leaders bearing the *gonfanon* or penant[41] are obviously not meant to be thrown, nor could be with any sensible result, and that in William of Poitiers' account of the battle, which is the best we have, Duke William finished the day with the stump of his broken lance in his hand.[42] Again, to the student of medieval military history, the wonder is not that so few Norman knights at Hastings in the Tapestry are couching their lances, but that any of them are;[43] for this technique, which will become the standard knightly practice, was developed especially as the means of unhorsing mounted opponents, of whom the Normans had none at Hastings. Nor is it a matter for surprise that the Normans on October 14, 1066, did not deliver the type of massed charge of the Royal Scots Greys at Waterloo, nor conduct themselves in the manner of the more sophisticated cavalry, say, of the thirteenth century; yet neither did they operate as an inchoate body of individuals. They fought in the *conrois*, the contingents, presumably, of individual lords and leaders bearing the *gonfanon*, whose members, by long training together, were very capable of acting together, and capable also, without doubt, of combination and co-ordination with other contingents. Such circum-

---

[37] Thus Glover, 12–16 – and the implication is, of course, that since there was no great difference between the two armies at Hastings, nor was there between the two societies that produced them.

[38] See, in addition to Lot, *L'art militaire* and the standard authorities, D. J. A. Ross, 'L'originalité de "Turoldus": le maniement de lance', in *Cahiers de Civilisation Médiévale*, vi. 1963.

[39] Thus Ordericus Vitalis' account (ed. Chibnall, ii. 30) of the accidental wounding of Hugh fitz Giroie by a lance carelessly thrown by his esquire in a training exercise. The date is *c.* 1040–60. In the same source, Richard de Heudicourt is struck in the back by the lance of a pursuing knight as he attempts to ford a river, the date being *c.* 1061–6 (ii. 132).

[40] Glover, 14, 15, 17. At Hastings on the Tapestry I can find only one certain instance of a lance, detached from any hand, in free flight from the Norman side towards the English (Fig. 62).

[41] Doc. 75.

[42] Ed. Foreville, 202.

[43] Fig. Figs. 60, 62, 65.

stances, for example, make the elaborate and disciplined tactic of the feigned flight at Hastings entirely feasible: it is, indeed, vouched for by all the main sources for the battle save the Bayeux Tapestry, is known to have been employed by the Normans (and others) elsewhere in this period, and has nothing against its credibility except the arrogant ignorance of those who still subscribe to the heresy that, all medieval warfare being chaos, all disciplined manoeuvres are *ipso facto* impossible.[44] Norman armies, which, for the English expedition of 1066 as in Italy,[45] went to the immense trouble of shipping their horses overseas, were unlikely to be mere mounted infantry in spirit and tactics, and it is finally to be urged that the very occasional portrayal by the Tapestry of a Norman knight fighting on foot at Hastings[46] in no wise supports the extraordinary interpretation placed upon it by Mr Glover, that 'The Norman . . . is so far from being a specialized cavalryman that he will cheerfully [*sic*] leap to the ground, let his horse trot free [*sic*], and mix it with the English on foot'.[47] The knight in such a predicament is likely to be neither cheerful nor happy, but to have been unhorsed by enemy action – as Duke William himself had in one account two, and in another three, horses killed under him in the battle, on each occasion fighting on until remounted, to the amazed admiration of his knights.[48]

Harold of England had at Hastings no cavalry, but only infantry, amongst whom the most professional and formidable element were the housecarls. William of Normandy had, in addition to a strong force of infantry including archers,[49] his cavalry, a specialist élite of knights (together with their apprentices, the young esquires, *tirones*, the *pueri* of the Tapestry).[50] The differences in composition and therefore in the tactics of the two armies point to the differences of the two societies which then met in arms, and militarily at Hastings, as in so many other ways, the Old World went down before the New. It may be a sick joke but it contains an element of truth to say that the English in 1066, as later in their history, sought to fight the last war once more. William of

---

[44] For the *conroi*, see J. F. Verbruggen, 'La tactique militaire des armées des chevaliers', *Revue du Nord*, xxix (1947). For both this subject and the feigned flight at Hastings, see Brown, *Normans*, 171–2 and n. 147.

[45] See D. P. Waley, 'Combined Operations in Sicily AD 1060–1078', *Papers of the British School of Rome*, xxii. 123. Cf. *Bayeux Tapestry*, ed. Stenton, Figs. 42–5.

[46] Figs. 66? 70? Cf. 67 for the loss of horses.

[47] P. 16.

[48] William of Poitiers, 198 (Doc. 27); *Carmen de Hastingae Proelio*, 40–2.

[49] Brown, *Normans*, 168–9. See especially William of Poitiers, 184 (Doc. 27). William the Conqueror, *pace* Hollister (*Military Organization of Norman England*, 127) did not need to learn the value of infantry from the English at Hastings.

[50] Ed. Stenton, Fig. 68 – a famous scene, with the rubric *Hie Odo episcopus . . . confortat pueros*.

Malmesbury, we have seen, thought that on the Breton expedition of 1064 William intended to demonstrate to Harold the superiority of the Norman sword (i.e. and cavalry) over the English battle-axe (i.e. and infantry).[51] The Bayeux Tapestry has a well-known illustration of the Norman duke on that same occasion conferring arms upon the English earl:[52] if, as seems most probable, this ceremony represents the conferment of knighthood,[53] there is deep significance in the fact that Harold, the leading magnate of the English realm, was not a knight before. In pre-Conquest England there was no cult of knighthood such as ensured that in Normandy all lords from the duke downwards were knights, nor were there any knights in England before 1066 save evidently Harold himself and those foreign knights, presumably, in the service of King Edward's 'Norman favourites', his nephew Earl Ralph of Hereford, Richard the son of Scrob, and others. But the Norman and French knights who dominate the battle scenes of Hastings on the Tapestry will dominate England afterwards, and because the defeated English saw them clattering and jingling through the countryside mainly in the train of the new Norman and French lords of the land, they applied to them the native word *cniht*, which meant servant or retainer.[54] Words and vocabulary, indeed, can come to our assistance again in echoing the nature of Old English society, for it appears that in England the Latin word *miles* did not finally change from the root, classical meaning of (any) soldier to the specialized, feudal meaning of knight, until the early twelfth century, a century later than was the case in Normandy and France.[55] There is, too, one other change, small but significant, in England as from 1066, which should be noted more often than it is. Every schoolboy knows that William as King of England adopted the two-faced pendant seal of Edward the Confessor. But whereas the last Old English king showed himself on both sides of his seal seated in majesty, the new Norman king, and all his successors after him, while retaining this representation on one side, showed themselves upon the other armed and mounted, that is as knights.[56] In this representation of themselves and their authority the kings were followed in due course by their lay magnates as soon as the latter began to have seals of their own. Such a change and development at the high and almost mystical

---

[51] Above, p. 39.

[52] Fig. 27.

[53] Wace in the twelfth century, it should be noted, thus interpreted the incident (*Roman de Rou*, ii. 372). Cf. Freeman, *Norman Conquest*, iii. 228; Round, *Feudal England*, 385. Glover, 8, has a contrary interpretation. For the ceremony of knighting at this time, see Brown, *Normans*, 47 and cf. n. 28 p. 27 above.

[54] Stenton, *First Century*, 132–5.

[55] See p. 27 and n. 29 above, with the references there given.

[56] See A. Wyon, *The Great Seals of England* (London, 1887), 3–7 and Pls. I, II. Doc. 77.

level of iconography, where symbolism matters most, points to a new element in English kingship and lordship alike, the potent element of feudalism.

2. *Absence of vassalic commendation*

The absence of cavalry in pre-Conquest English armies right down to Hastings in 1066 is thus itself a proof of the absence of knights, knighthood and chivalry, and therefore, one might add at once, of feudalism. Unfortunately, however, it is necessary to go on and argue not only the absence of the knight, but also the presence or absence of those other fundamentals of feudalism, namely vassalic commendation, the knight's fee, and the castle. As for the first of these, while in the absence of anything comparable to Ganshof's continental researches the Cloud of Unknowing, shot with attendant controversy,[57] hangs over Old English commendation, the overall pattern is nevertheless clear enough. Without the evolution of a specialist military and social élite of knights, we should not expect to find that specialized type of commendation which in France, the Low Countries and the Rhineland developed to distinguish the honourable and voluntary bonds which bound that class together from the increasingly dishonourable and hereditary bonds that bound the serfs or peasants to their masters and the land.[58] Of course we meet with commendation in pre-Conquest England (though it may well be significant that there is no noun or substantive for it before 1066)[59] as we meet with lordship, but both are of the original and basic Germanic kind from which feudal or vassalic commendation and feudal lordship had subsequently developed on the Continent. We thus find in Old English society the 'hold-oath' whereby a man promises to be faithful to his lord, shunning what he shuns and loving what he loves,[60] and this appears to be the equivalent of the continental oath of fealty, significantly the oldest, least specific and least important element in Frankish commendation.[61] We hear sometimes also of 'bowing' to a

---

[57] The principal literature upon the subject of the Old English commendation is, Maitland, *Domesday Book and Beyond*, 98–104; C. Stephenson, 'Commendation and related problems in Domesday Book', *English Historical Review*, lix (1944); B. Dodwell, 'East Anglian Commendation', ibid., lxiii (1948); Edward Miller, *The Abbey and Bishopric of Ely* (Cambridge, 1951), Chapter III, especially 59–63.

[58] Above, p. 29.

[59] Maitland, 116; Stephenson, *English Historical Review*, lix. 290. It is also worth noting that there is no vernacular, Anglo-Saxon noun as the equivalent of the Latin and feudal *fidelis* for the person who has commended himself (F. E. Harmer, *Anglo-Saxon Writs*, Manchester, 1952, 54).

[60] Maitland, 98–9; J. E. A. Jolliffe, *Constitutional History of Medieval England*, (London, 1937), 79–80; Dodwell, *English Historical Review*, lxiii. 305; Stubbs, *Select Charters*, 74. Docs. 13, 59.

[61] Bloch, 146–51.

lord,[62] but if words have any meaning this cannot be the crucial and distinguishing element of vassalic commendation, the act of homage, the *immixtio manuum*, whereby the vassal is created. The very word 'vassal', if it appears in pre-Conquest English sources, evidently does so only as an obvious borrowing without significance.[63] Nor do we hear of investiture with the fief, nor could we since, as we shall see, there was no fief.[64] The hold-oath and bowing are all we seem to have. In short, in the absence in England of a new knightly class of lords and vassals no exclusive and particular ceremony appropriate to them had developed from the ancient, basic and undifferentiated forms of Germanic commendation, and this for our purposes matters more than whatever conclusion may emerge from current controversy over the precise nature of the tie established by Old English commendation – whether it is strong or fragile (Maitland's 'mere commendation'), purely personal or inherent in the land.[65]

Nevertheless these matters are relevant to our purpose because of their significance. In France, the Low Countries and the Rhineland the development in the ninth and tenth centuries of an exclusive, vassalic commendation is one manifestation of the evolution of a new specialist warrior class, and a new social ruling class of knights, tending to monopolize not only military worth but also the concept of social and legal freedom, as the peasant's military importance wanes and he himself sinks towards servitude. It is a manifestation, thus, of hardening class distinctions, between knights and peasants – with the bourgeoisie uncomfortably different from both, and the clergy different again (though as individuals, closely associated with all three). Language illuminates once more, for as the true slave disappears in feudal Europe the peasant inevitably takes his place at the bottom of the social hierarchy and becomes the serf: the Latin word *servus*, once meaning 'slave', is applied to him.[66] But in England in these as in other matters an older

[62] Jolliffe, 79; Maitland, 347; Dodwell, 305. For a famous instance dating from just after the Conquest, note the description of the Salisbury Oath of 1086 in the Anglo-Saxon Chronicle 'E' – 'and all bowed down to him (*ealle hi bugon to him*) and became his men and swore oaths of fealty (*holdathas*) to him': Stubbs, *Select Charters*, 96; Doc. 13. In the edition of Whitelock (162) the technicalities of 'bowing' and 'holdoaths' are obscured by the translation. For an earlier instance from 901, cited by Jolliffe, the men with Æthelwold who in Whitelock's translation had 'given allegiance to him' (59) had in fact and literally 'bowed to him' [*gebugon*]: see Plummer, *Two of the Saxon Chronicles Parallell*, i, 92.

[63] Bloch, 181; Maitland, 347, n. 1. The lady who, in Maitland (98), 'put herself with her land in the hand of the queen' (a doubtful reference to homage in any case) did so explicitly in the time of King William.

[64] Below, p. 61.

[65] For this controversy, see p. 43, n. 57 above.

[66] Bloch, 260–1.

world survived down to 1066. Slaves survived, significantly, in considerable numbers,[67] and the 'ceorl', the peasant, whatever his individual circumstances, remained a free man at law, retaining also, so far as we can tell, a worthy place in war.[68] In law a man's legal status was still determined by the ancient Germanic concept of the *wergeld* or bloodprice, not by the harsh reality of military proficiency and economic function.[69] We may take with a pinch of salt the nostalgic evocation of the Good Old Days implicit and explicit in that curious compilation on social status, 'Of People's Ranks and Laws', emanating from early eleventh-century England, but its author (probably Archbishop Wulfstan of York) thought it a good thing that a ceorl who prospered should become a thegn, and likewise a merchant also.[70] In feudal Europe we have to wait centuries for a knighted grocer, and have not (one would guess) achieved a knighted peasant even yet. Of course, in England on the eve of the Norman Conquest there was a huge gulf between the great earl at one extreme and Hod the less prosperous peasant at the other, but in between degrees were imprecise. Marc Bloch, finding the condition of the peasant classes in mid-eleventh-century England irresistibly reminiscent of that prevailing in late Carolingian Gaul two centuries before, spoke also of a 'sort of confusion of classes'.[71] His words are echoed by Edward Miller, who writes of 'the luxuriant confusion of Old English society',[72] and finds, on the basis of his Ely evidence at least, that the true answer to the controversial nature of the tie of pre-Conquest commendation is that it varied almost indefinitely in strength and character according to the infinite variety of individual cases.[73] In short, we reach the same conclusion, and confirm it, by another route: Old English commendation reflects, as it is bound to do, the nature of Old English society; and the absence of vassalic commendation points to the absence of feudalism.

3. *Absence of the fief*

No native knights, then, in pre-Conquest England, and (and in consequence) no knightly, vassalic commendation. In such circumstances we should not expect to find the fief, that is the knight's fee, designed for his support and bestowed upon him by investiture in the three-fold ceremony of feudal commendation – an obvious point yet one to which

---

[67] See H. R. Loyn, *Anglo-Saxon England and the Norman Conquest* (London, 1962), 87, 350–3.
[68] Below, p. 50.
[69] Bloch, 183–4, 284; Stenton, *First Century*, 5, 129–30. See also p. 81 below.
[70] *English Historical Documents*, i. 432; Stubbs, *Select Charters*, 88; Doc. 60.
[71] Bloch, 184, 270.
[72] Miller, *Abbey and Bishopric of Ely*, 74.
[73] Ibid., 60.

historians of English feudalism, Maitland not least, have often seemed peculiarly blind.[74] The point becomes even more obvious if we define the fee, which is a parcel of land held by a knight as the vassal and tenant of his lord (who may be, but more often is not, the king or prince) in return for military service (the crucial service amongst others), and more specifically military knight-service, to that lord. Yet unfortunately so much has been written on the fief and its origins in England that we cannot leave the subject so, but must put and answer the question for ourselves and, as it were, in its own right: namely, can the knight's fee, or anything like it, be found in the pre-Conquest period? The question involves military organization and land tenure, and there is no doubt of its fundamental relevance to our purpose, for feudalism is much concerned with both, and, as we have seen, in fact the very words feudal and feudalism are derived from the Latin *feudum* meaning fief. We may begin therefore by noting that the word *feudum* does not appear in England until after 1066,[75] and we may well end by taking our stand upon J. E. A. Jolliffe's aphorism that 'because the English had not the fee, they also had not feudalism'.[76] For the rest, for the bibliography of this particular controversy upon which English-speaking historians have expended a disproportionate amount of their energies, we shall principally need, on the one hand J. H. Round followed by F. M. Stenton,[77] and, on the other, Maitland[78] and his latter-day supporters Marjory Hollings[79] and Eric John,[80] together with the most recent survey of Anglo-Saxon and Anglo-Norman military organization by Professor C. W. Hollister.[81]

On the subject of Old English military organization the familiar Cloud of Unknowing at once descends. 'No matter with which we have to deal,' wrote Maitland, 'is darker than the constitution of the English army on the eve of its defeat,'[82] and his words are echoed by Hollister's recent warning 'that the whole subject of Anglo-Saxon military organi-

---

[74] E.g. Maitland, 196, 199, 307, 363. Cf. above, p. 31 and below, p. 58.

[75] Maitland, 373.

[76] J. E. A. Jolliffe, *Constitutional History of Medieval England*, 78.

[77] 'The Introduction of Knight Service into England', printed in Round's *Feudal England*, and Stenton, *First Century of English Feudalism*, especially Chapter IV.

[78] *Domesday Book and Beyond*, 194–201, 354–75.

[79] Marjory Hollings, 'The Survival of the five-hide unit in the Western Midlands', *English Historical Review*, lxiii (1948). An abbreviated version of this essay is incorporated in the Introduction to her edition of *The Red Book of Worcester* for the Worcestershire Historical Society, 4 vols., 1934–50.

[80] *Land Tenure in Early England* (Leicester, 1961), Chapters V to VIII, especially Chapter VIII.

[81] Respectively *Anglo-Saxon Military Institutions on the Eve of the Norman Conquest* and *The Military Organization of Norman England*.

[82] P. 194.

zation is notoriously difficult and obscure, and that few if any conclusions can be reached that are much more than tentative'.[83] Nevertheless, as so often seems to be the case with Anglo-Saxon history, though we know next to nothing about the details the main outline appears to be clear. Almost the only piece of direct evidence we have, a clause of the Laws of Ine of Wessex, dating from the late seventh century, refers to military service, that is service in the *fyrd* or army, as obligatory upon all classes of free men, namely *gesiths*, or nobles, with and without land, and ceorls or peasants, default being punishable by a penalty payment or *wite* (thus *fyrdwite*) scaled according to the rank of the defaulter.[84] This universal obligation to military service upon all the free men (not slaves) is what we should expect of early Germanic society and find in Frankish Gaul as well as England.[85] In England the principle survived the Conquest, as in France it survived the growth of feudalism to continue as the *arrière ban*, and in a sense it still survives in Western nations whenever conscription is applied. In pre-Conquest England also military service appears at least from the late eighth century as part of the 'three-fold necessity', the so-called *Trimoda Necessitas*, i.e. the triple common burdens of fyrd-service, work upon bridges and work upon burghs or public defences, which lay upon all free men[86] – or in practice, as we must now see, came to lie upon all the land. For to be organized such services, military and other, need to be assessed: sooner or later one will need to know how many and how much is due from any given district. But early government finds it difficult or impossible to deal with individuals, who come and go, grow old, sick, and die, and vary in sex as well as age. One is concerned with adult males; one is likely to place the responsibility upon the heads of households; it is easier to count or estimate households or homesteads than heads.

Thus the obligations become territorialized and one can dimly see how. Bede in the seventh century tells us that the hide was that amount of land (it will vary therefore in extent and even value according to other circumstances) sufficient to support a peasant household: by the late Old English period the hide was the universal, artificial unit of assessment for the exaction of taxes (the geld) and services all over 'English' and 'hidated' England – the carucate or ploughland evidently fulfilling the same role in the Danelaw and Scandinavianized districts.[87] Such

[83] *Military Organization of Norman England*, 14.
[84] Stubbs, *Select Charters*, 68; *English Historical Documents*, i. 370; Doc. 56. For the *gesith*, see above, p. 34.
[85] See e.g. F. Lot, *L'art militaire*, i. 74–5; Hollister, *Anglo-Saxon Military Institutions*, 27.
[86] See W. H. Stevenson, 'Trinoda Necessitas', *English Historical Review*, xxix, (1914), and Eric John, *Land Tenure*, 78.
[87] For the *sulungs* of Kent and the *leets* of East Anglia, see Hollister, *Anglo-Saxon Military Institutions*, 52–3.

services, it must be emphasized, were royal services, national services, as the geld was a national tax paid to the King by free subjects, and were thus organized from the top downwards, through the shires and their subdivisions of hundreds (in English England, and perhaps in origin a hundred hides) and wapentakes (in the Danelaw), and upon each vill and individual estate therein, each assessed at so many hides or carucates. In this way, then, Anglo-Saxon fyrd-service, like the other national services, became territorialized, and we can say, if we like, that military service in the late Old English state had become territorial rather than personal[88] – just as we can also say that in feudal society the knight-service of a vassal to his lord is personal in the beginning but is territorialized if and when the vassal is enfeoffed and owes service thereafter in return for his fief. This, however, is, to say the least, a very slender common factor and should cause no confusion between the two systems, national and feudal: on the one hand a uniform system of military service, a national levy, owed to the King by subjects and lying upon all the land irrespective of who holds it and of whom it is held, and on the other a series of arbitrary tenurial bargains between individuals whereby, in respect of the fee held of him, the vassal owes military service to his lord, who may be, but more often is not, the King or Prince. Far from confusion there is contrast, which becomes yet sharper if we remember, as continually we must, that feudal vassalage and investiture produced knight-service, cavalry, while Anglo-Saxon fyrd-service produced infantry if the fyrd went by land, and some sort of sea-borne warrior if the fyrd went by sea – as in the late Old English period it very often did.[89] It is difficult to think of anything military yet less feudal than a marine, or, for that matter, a navy and a sea-fyrd.

At this point we must introduce certain complications. In the first place, it is generally agreed that at some stage, and presumably in the interests of quality rather than quantity, the rate of assessment for military service in England was reduced from one man from every hide to one man from a number of hides. The earliest reference to anything of the kind occurs in a charter of King Coenwulf of Mercia of c.801, confirming an earlier grant of an estate of thirty hides which is to be subject to the *trimoda necessitas* but in the case of military expeditions to send five men only.[90] This looks like a rate of one man from every six hides, but in the well-known passage relating to Berkshire in Domesday Book the rate is one man from every five hides – 'If the King sent an army anywhere, only one soldier went from five hides, and four shillings were given him from each hide as subsistence and wages for two

---

[88] For confusion on this point, see Hollister, ibid. 2.
[89] See Hollister, *ut supra*, 103ff; cf. Eric John, 119ff.
[90] See Hollister, 61. The charter is No. 201 in W. de G. Birch, *Cartularium Saxonicum* (London, 1885–93), vol. i.

months'.[91] Though Stenton warned against the dangers of generalizing from the particular in this instance and deducing from this Berkshire evidence that a five-hide rule applied over all 'English', i.e. hidated, England, there is a good deal of evidence from Domesday and elsewhere, which Round was amongst the first to emphasize, to suggest that it did, with an equivalent six-carucate rule for the Danelaw and areas of Scandinavian influence.[92] We also have an instructive Continental and Carolingian analogy, where out of the ancient obligation upon all free men to military service there evolved the custom under Charlemagne and his immediate successors of summoning infantry soldiers at the rate of one man for every four manses – the manse here being a concept equivalent to the hide.[93] In any event, we thus meet the 'five-hide unit' of pre-Conquest English military organization, and we may perhaps anticipate by remarking that the more universal it was in practice, the less feudal such a uniform system may seem. Meanwhile if there is less than unanimity amongst historians about the universality of the five-hide and six-carucate rule, so is there about its application, Stenton seeming to suggest that the selective principle replaced the older obligation of one man from every hide,[94] while Hollister argues for the retention of the 'Great Fyrd', the levy of all able-bodied men, for local defence in an emergency, alongside the 'Select Fyrd' (the terms are his) for more sophisticated and distant operations.[95] It seems likely that Hollister is right, if only because it is clear that the ancient obligation upon all free men to take up arms in case of need was never lost in English history,[96] though he would no doubt be the first to admit that the evidence simply will not allow us to be too precise about the details of Old English military organization, nor should we seek to impose too tidy a pattern upon a society by no means unified in 1066 and one of whose features was, in the memorable phrase of Edward Miller, 'luxuriant confusion'.[97]

The same phrase may help us to decide the next issue of disagreement touching 'the constitution of the English army on the eve of its defeat', namely whether the typical warrior produced by the fyrd-system – more precisely, to follow Hollister's terminology, for the 'Select Fyrd' – was a thegn,[98] or whether, as Stenton insists, such service was only for peasants while the thegn served under an obligation no less ancient but different, one which was 'purely personal . . . a duty which follows from

[91] *Domesday Book*, Record Commission ed. (London, 1783), i. 56b. Doc. 70.
[92] Stenton, *First Century*, 117; cf. Round, *Feudal England*, 44ff; Hollister, Chapter III.
[93] Cf. Hollister, 42–3.
[94] *Anglo-Saxon England*, 286–8, 575.
[95] Hollister, 26ff.
[96] Hollister, 27; above, p. 47.
[97] Miller, *Abbey and Bishopric of Ely*, 74; above, p. 45.
[98] Hollister, 80.

D

his rank, the expression of the traditions of an order which, as a class, represented the military companions of a lord, the *gesithas* of ancient times'.[99] The distinction may seem too precise (just as Stenton's notion that the thegn received a personal summons may seem administratively implausible at this date) and in the nature of things we might expect that either the peasant or the thegn might serve, in accordance with local and particular circumstances. Stenton is certainly justified in emphasizing the surviving aristocratic military traditions of the thegnhood in which Anglo-Saxon literature is steeped, but it has also been pointed out before now that some of the most noble sentiments in the poem of the battle of Maldon (991) are uttered by a simple ceorl,[100] and there is no evidence to suggest that the Old English peasantry as a class was not still regarded as 'fyrd-worthy' in the first half of the eleventh century. The most detailed modern discussion of the point will be found in Hollister,[101] whose argument carries conviction and whose conclusion must therefore be accepted, namely that 'the typical select-fyrd warrior'[102] was the thegn, though the more prosperous peasant would also serve upon occasion, not least because there were not enough thegns to go round. Stenton's contention that a universal and personal obligation to military service, distinct from the territorial obligation of the fyrd, lay upon the thegnhood as a class, can only be sustained, for example, if it can be shown that all thegns in the event did so serve, whereas in fact we have evidence that they did not – as with the case of Siwate and his three brothers in Lincolnshire, who, in the time of King Edward, shared their late father's estate equally between them, and shared also the military burden after the fashion of the Berkshire custom in Domesday, in that only one of them served for the whole estate, receiving financial support from his brothers to do so.[103] It must be admitted also that the positive evidence cited by Stenton to prove his contention fails to do so, whether we read and construe the 'most important' piece from the Worcestershire section of Domesday or the famous Berkshire Domesday entry which is used to support it.[104] In the first case the passage (as so often) is concerned with default of service rather than with the service itself, and its most natural rendering would seem to be simply that the penalty for such default, in accordance with the normal principle of Anglo-Saxon and Germanic law, was scaled in proportion to the rank of the defaulter[105] – not that the passage is concerned exclusively with some unique obligation of thegns. The word

[99] *First Century*, 116–19.
[100] Hollister, p. 75. Doc. 18.   [101] Pp. 63ff.   [102] P. 80.
[103] See Hollister, 69 and *Domesday Book*, i. 375b.
[104] See *First Century*, 118 n. 1, citing *Domesday Book*, i. 172 for Worcestershire and i. 56b for Berkshire. Docs. 69, 70.
[105] Thus Ine's Law touching fyrdwyte, cited p. 47 above. Doc. 56.

'thegn' is not used, but we are told that a defaulter of high social standing, an independent landowner of status (in the terminology of the Confessor's day, 'if he is so free a man as to have *soc* and *sac* [rights of jurisdiction] and can go with his land to whom he pleases'), may forfeit all his land to the king, whereas a lesser man, a man of lesser independence, 'the freeman of another lord', will get off with a fine of 40s. As for the Berkshire passage, it seems arbitrary and unwarranted to divide into two distinct parts what seems one integrated whole, and make the first part (the first two sentences) relate to the territorial fyrd-service of the peasant, and the second part (the last two sentences) relate to a separate personal obligation of the thegn. There is also the *Rectitudines Singularum Personarum*, a pre-Conquest document purporting to list the rights and obligations of the various classes of Old English society, which is surely unequivocal in making the thegn's military duty territorial like everyone else's, a part of the *trimoda necessitas* owed '*in respect of his land*'.[106]

It may well be that there is a certain unreality about these discussions if we seek to apply them to the heat and burden of the day, to wars and rumours of wars, for as Stenton observes, 'It is more than probable that many thegns of the eleventh century were country gentlemen, with no special aptitude for war'.[107] By the late Old English period the rank and status was hereditary, and also we have already noted prosperous peasants and successful merchants rising to it.[108] Certainly early history seems to reveal a repeating pattern of a warrior aristocracy, subsequently planted out upon the land as its reward, becoming thereby less effective as a military force, and thus in due course and of necessity replaced. In this way in England the thegns had taken the place of the *gesiths* and by the eleventh century had themselves largely given way to the housecarls as the élite military force, prevented, we may suppose, only by the Norman Conquest and its new ruling class of knights from becoming established on the land as a new warrior aristocracy.[109] As things were, it is clear that, whatever the detailed organization and efficacy of the Anglo-Saxon fyrd-system, the best troops and the professional element in Old English armies on the eve of the Conquest were provided by what it is now fashionable amongst historians to call mercenary forces but who, because of the modern disapproving connotations of the word 'mercenary', are better thought of as what they were, the housecarls of the hearth-troops, the personal retainers of the military households of the king and earls.[110] The 'feudal' forces of eleventh-century France,

---

[106] *English Historical Documents*, ii. 813; Doc. 61. Cf. Hollister, 70.
[107] *First Century*, 119.
[108] Above, p. 45.
[109] Above, p. 34.
[110] Hollister, 9ff.

Normandy and Anglo-Norman England similarly, i.e. knights serving in return for their fiefs, were heavily reinforced by stipendary troops, both unenfeoffed knights and other ranks (for in military matters, feudalism like patriotism, is not enough), but this factor common to both, like the central role of the military household in the organization of each, does not make the two systems, national and feudal, the same, any more than the fact that the best armed warriors on each side wore mail in battle makes the two sides identical.

In fact we have so far discussed and analysed Old English military organization without finding anything feudal about it, still less have we found the fief as an element in that organization. To follow Maitland and the modern critics of the established view in the attempt to find the fief and with it feudalism in pre-Conquest England, we have to introduce one more complication, that of the franchise or liberty, into the organiz-ation of fyrd-service, and also look at the forms of land-ownership and land-tenure in England, more especially the lease. We shall also and very soon have to turn to one particular district, to the western midlands, the bishopric of Worcester, and the liberty of Oswaldslow, whence almost all the alleged evidence is said to come, and upon which, therefore, almost all the argument in favour of pre-Conquest English feudalism is based.

A problem common to all early government is that of getting one's will carried out at a distance, of administering the provinces. Two stan-dard medieval responses to this problem, applied in combination, were the itinerary, whereby the king or prince (and lesser lords similarly in their lesser spheres), by moving continually about his realm with much of the apparatus of government in his itinerant household, can deal with affairs direct, and the liberty or franchise whereby royal powers and rights (which are also profitable) are delegated to a local lord on the spot. Further, while secular lords will frequently hold greater or lesser franchises, ecclesiastical lords were particularly favoured by the delega-tion of royal rights and powers, partly no doubt because this could be regarded simply as a good thing, there being a strong theocratic element in early medieval government, but also for reasons of sheer practicality, prelates (bishops and abbots), being educated men with the capacity of literacy, and with the nucleus of a literate bureaucracy about them. In this way many, perhaps most, perhaps all, lords of any substance, secular or ecclesiastical, in pre-Conquest England had rights of juris-diction (*sac* and *soc* – cf. the Worcestershire Domesday entry cited above),[111] usually regarded by historians as delegated, franchisal juris-diction: many hundreds were in private hands, administered by, and their courts presided over by, the bailiffs and officials of the lord; while the greater and more privileged liberties, frequently attached to

[111] Above, p. 51 and Doc. 69.

churches, like those of the abbots of Bury St Edmunds or Ely – or that of the Bishop of Worcester – comprised in effect large districts, and/or large numbers of men (for the two did not always coincide), governed and administered by the lord and his officials, albeit on the King's behalf.[112] The lord of such a franchise, or any lord thus privileged, would exact and organize royal services on the King's behalf, including it might be (which is the point for us) military service in the fyrd. How far in practice down the scale of lordship the liberty of fyrd-service extended is less clear, and also less relevant to our purpose; but Stenton is obviously right to point to the responsibility at any rate of many thegns for the military service of those under them, for this is implicit in the Worcestershire Domesday passage relating to the fyrd, as it is also in the laws of Cnut who, insisting that 'fyrd-wite' (i.e. the penalty payment for default) is a royal right (naturally since fyrd-service is a royal service), nevertheless adds 'unless he [the king] will honour any man more highly', i.e. unless the right is delegated to a lord.[113]

As for landholding in pre-Conquest England, it is known to us in three forms, folk-land (evidently the normality for ordinary men), book-land (a privileged form bequeathed by and held under 'land-book' or charter) and lease-hold tenure. Into the arguments and controversies about the precise nature of the first two, we fortunately need not go,[114] for no one has ever suggested that they were feudal. They are, rather, pre-feudal, forms however circumscribed and qualified of real ownership, without any necessary implications of lordship, of the tenure by one man from another. In feudal France such land survived here and there as the *allod*, like pockets of resistance holding out from an older world – but not, it is to be noted, in post-Conquest England, where the pure feudal doctrine of *nulle terre sans seigneur* was implicit from the beginning in the sheer facts of conquest and the Conqueror's control of the subsequent land settlement. Lease-hold tenure, however, is another matter.[115] It is a form of tenure, and of conditional tenure, and it involves land-lordship of its very nature since it is land held by one man from another. It has, then, these points in common with the fee: add that leasehold land may be held in return for, on condition of,

[112] Thus, as a touch of living reality, the eight and a half hundreds of the medieval liberty of St Edmund still survive in the guise of West Suffolk, administered from Bury St Edmunds as a unit of local government separate from East Suffolk, administered from Ipswich.

[113] Stenton, *First Century*, e.g. 118 n. 1, 127; *Domesday Book*, i. 172; Doc. 69; Cnut II, Secular Dooms, cc. 12, 15, in Stubbs, *Select Charters*, 86, and *English Historical Documents*, i. 420. Doc. 58.

[114] For a convenient summary, see H. R. Loyn, *Anglo-Saxon England and the Norman Conquest*, 170ff.

[115] The best treatment of the whole subject of the Old English lease, which survives the Conquest, will be found in Chapter VI of R. Lennard, *Rural England, 1086–1135* (Oxford, 1959).

services to the landlord, and one can see why so much attention is focused upon it by the would-be feudalists of pre-Conquest England. It is as well, therefore, to note at the outset that in pre-Conquest England it is book-land and folk-land that are the basic forms of land holding, not leasehold land which is exceptional, and as Maitland himself observed, without the Norman Conquest 'we have no reason for believing that . . . the formula of dependent tenure would ever have got hold of every acre of English land . . . The law of "land loans" . . . would hardly have become our only land law.'[116] There is no mystery about the Old English lease or *laen* (i.e. 'loan', hence 'laen-land' is land loaned and held by lease) since like a modern lease it conveys property for a limited term, in Anglo-Saxon England usually for one or more lives, in return for specified rent, or, in this period, services. Lease and fief thus have certain similarities and common factors: both involve land held in return for service to a lord; neither is hereditary (though a long lease for a term of three lives, for example, approaches closer to it than the early fief); both could be called by the old word 'benefice', *beneficium*, though on the Continent a new word 'fief', *feudum, feodum*, has by now been coined for what is rightly regarded as a new thing;[117] both also were a valuable means whereby landowners could make grants of land without losing it, retaining superiority, lordship and evential reversion. But there the similarity ceases and the analogy can be pushed no further. The archetype of the fief which we must have in order to be feudal is the knight's fee, the *feudum militis*, the *fief de haubert*: the crucial element, the core and essence, of that is military service, more specifically, knight-service, by the tenant to the lord of the fee: of this there is no sign in any extant Old English lease – the vital point, to emerge more fully when we turn, as everybody turns, to the bulk of the surviving evidence from the bishopric of Worcester and the liberty of Oswaldslow.

As we turn to the bishopric of Worcester and Oswaldslow, there are two preliminary points to be made. The first is, that even if it could be shown that proto-feudalism, or feudalism, or (if Eric John is to be believed)[118] an already obsolescent feudalism, existed here before the Conquest, it would still be a classic and reckless instance of generalizing from the particular to go on to assume that all England was feudal, though this explicitly or implicitly is the argument of Maitland and his modern followers. The second point is that the district falls within the western midlands of England, an area noted for its conservatism,[119] which makes it a very unlikely candidate for the accolade of pre-

[116] *Domesday Book and Beyond*, 211.
[117] Cf. Ganshof, *Feudalism*, 96–7.
[118] *Land Tenure in early England*, 160.
[119] See J. O. Prestwich, 'Anglo-Norman Feudalism and the Problem of Continuity', *Past and Present*, No. 26 (1963), 44.

Conquest English feudalism since in the time-scale and historical sequence of Western Europe and Latin Christendom feudalism in the tenth and eleventh centuries was, so to speak, the latest thing. Next we must note two introductory, non-controversial but very basic facts. The triple hundred of Oswaldslow, three hundreds grouped together, was a liberty or franchise, highly privileged, held by the Bishops of Worcester, and originally granted, it is thought, by King Edgar to St Oswald, Bishop of Worcester (961–992) in 964.[120] And within Oswaldslow, as also outside it, Oswald and his predecessors and successors, like other prelates elsewhere in this period, had leased lands to tenants (almost invariably at Worcester for a term of three lives, i.e. the grantee and two heirs or successors) in return for various rents and services.[121] There is thus nothing unusual either about Oswaldslow or these arrangements: what is unusual is the amount of relevant evidence which has survived, chiefly in Hemming's eleventh-century cartulary of the church of Worcester, printed by Hearne in the early eighteenth century and, curiously, never yet re-edited.[122] That evidence comprises the remarkable series of leases themselves, extending overall from the eighth to the eleventh century,[123] a formal letter or memorandum by St Oswald to King Edgar setting down the terms on which his leases collectively had been issued,[124] and thus more important for our purposes than the leases themselves,[125] and the so-called Domesday 'cartula' of 1086,[126] the return touching Oswaldslow drawn up by or for the Conqueror's commissioners on the testimony of the men of Worcestershire, duly entered and summarized in Domesday Book itself.[127]

The crucial question has been concisely, if somewhat truculently, put by Eric John – 'What is at issue is whether *laen*-tenure at Worcester was dependent military tenure, whether in other words *laens* were fees

[120] A charter, the so-called 'Altitonantis' charter, purporting to grant it survives in a twelfth-century version. This is certainly a fabrication to some extent, and may be entirely so. For an exhaustive discussion in its favour, see Eric John, *Land Tenure*, 90ff, who also prints a revised and improved edition of the text as Appendix I, 162–6. But for continuing doubts, see R. R. Darlington, *Cartulary of Worcester Cathedral Priory*, Pipe Roll Society, N.S. 38 (London, 1968), xiii–xix. The charter is No. 1135 in Birch, *Cartularium Saxonicum*.

[121] See Lennard, *Rural England*, 159; N. R. Ker, 'Hemming's Cartulary: a description of the two Worcester cartularies in Cotton Tiberius A. xiii', in *Studies in Medieval History presented to F. M. Powicke* (Oxford, 1948), 69.

[122] *Hemmingi Chartularium Ecclesiae Wigornensis*, ed. Thomas Hearne (Oxford, 1723).

[123] See Lennard and Ker as above. Docs. 43, 44.

[124] Hemming, *Chartularium*, i, 292 (where it is called '*Indiculum*' in the heading). This is No. 1136 in Birch. Doc. 42.

[125] For Maitland (p. 358) it was 'for our purposes the most important of all the documents that have come down to us from the age before the Conquest'.

[126] Also called *Indiculum* in Hemming, i. 287. Doc. 65.

[127] *Domesday Book*, i. 172b; in Hemming, i. 72 amd 298. Doc. 66.

as Maitland and St Wulfstan thought.'[128] Though Maitland may have thought so, it is very clear that Wulfstan (Bishop of Worcester 1062–95) did not, as we shall see, while Oswald who granted so many of the leases may well have never heard of fees. The leases themselves are frequently granted to thegns, many of the grantees being described as *ministri*, the usual Latin rendering of thegns.[129] Some grantees are described as *cnihts*,[130] that is unspecified servants or retainers of the bishop,[131] others as *milites*, that is unspecified soldiers and not, *pace* Maitland, at this date in England and without further evidence, 'knights'.[132] One at least was a nobleman of distinction,[133] and some are the bishop's kinsmen.[134] Since military service is the issue, it is to be noted that some of the grantees are priests, clerks and deacons,[135] and one or two are women.[136] Save for a rare reference to a distinctly un-knightly and unfeudal agricultural service,[137] the leases make no reference to future service to the Bishop in return for the land, still less to military service to him, still less to knightly service – which would be a startling omission from any post-Conquest charter of enfeoffment[138] – but are content with unspecific conditions of obedience and subjection.[139] The oft-quoted lease of Bishop Ealdred (1046–62) to one Wulfgeat, for example, cited by Eric John in support of his thesis that *laens* are fees,[140] does not specifically mention military service at all. The grant is of 1½ hides at Ditchford for three lives: Wulfgeat and his two successors 'shall always be submissive and obedient and acknowledge the lordship of whoever is bishop at the time'; and at the end of the lease, as a kind of postscript, it is added that 'at the king's summons the holder shall discharge the obligations on these 1½ hides at the rate of one [hide]'. Here then is an instance of 'beneficial hidation' (which is the point of the added note) – the assessment of the estate is here reduced from 1½ hides to one, and at this rate in the future what are clearly royal services ('at the king's summons') are to be discharged, these services including no doubt the *trimoda necessitas* of fyrd-service, bridge-work and borough-work,

---

[128] *Land Tenure*, 145.
[129] E.g. Hemming, i. 123, 127, 128, 130, 133 and *passim*. Cf. Maitland, 357; Stenton *First Century*, 126 and n.
[130] E.g. i. 151, 163, 178 (respectively Nos. LVI, LV, XLVI, with translations in A. J. Robertson, *Anglo-Saxon Charters* (Cambridge, 1939).
[131] Cf. above, p. 42.
[132] Hemming, i. 122, 191, 210. Cf. Maitland, 357, and above, p. 42.
[133] i. 166 (*cuidam inter primates hujus regni nobilissimo, nomine Aethelmundo*).
[134] E.g. i. 147, 153, 174, 212.
[135] E.g. i. 135, 138, 139, 240.
[136] i. 170, 186.
[137] i. 208
[138] See p. 71 below.
[139] Cf. Maitland, 357–8.
[140] Robertson, *Anglo-Saxon Charters*, No. CXI; *Land Tenure*, 147. Doc. 44.

though this is not stated but taken for granted. Which brings us to the point. Military service is only mentioned in the Worcester leases in terms of the reservation of the *trimoda necessitas*; the lease will frequently state, as does that of Oswald to 'a certain cleric whose name is Goding', that 'this estate . . . shall be free from every duty of a secular nature except the repair of bridges and fortifications and military service against enemies (*contra hostes expeditionem*)'.[141] But in pre-Conquest England this three-fold common obligation was a royal service. The military service it includes is in no sense owed to the bishop as their lord by his lease-hold tenants as a condition of their tenure: the case is simply that within his liberty the Bishop has the duty and the privilege of exacting royal services on the King's behalf. To put the matter another way, fyrd-service, borough-work and bridge-work lay upon all the land of England, owed to the King, and would have so lain and been so owed within Oswaldslow whether or not the district was a franchise of the Bishop and whether or not the land therein was leased to the Bishop's tenants. No doubt St Oswald had also in Oswaldslow the fines for default of service, as he was also evidently expected to lead, in person or by deputy, its contingent to the fyrd and could thus be called by the title of *archiductor*.[142]

In any event the military service is the King's, and not the Bishop's save in his role (almost an office) of franchise-holder. The point is crucial, and is also made entirely plain by our other documentary evidence. Within Oswaldslow, states the Domesday 'cartula' of 1086, the bishop has 'both the king's service and his own' (*et regis servicium et suum*),[143] and the same distinction is drawn by St Oswald in his own memorandum about his own leases. Having listed the services which the tenants owe the Bishop as a condition of their leases, the memorandum goes on to state that they are to do all other things necessary to fulfil 'both his [the bishop's] service and the king's' (*sive ad suum servitium sive ad regale explendum*).[144] And the services which the lease-hold tenants owe to the Bishop personally as their land-lord, set out in the document, are, as is well known, miscellaneous and non-military.[145] As though this were not enough, the Domesday commissioners, enquiring into the very matter of the leases in Oswaldslow, and in the time of St Wulfstan, and no doubt on the testimony of St Wulfstan, state

---

[141] Robertson, No. LXI, p. 127; in Hemming, i. 139–41, and cf. e.g. pp. 125, 126, and *passim*.

[142] In the 'Altitonantis' charter (John, 164) and in Oswald's *Memorandum* (Hemming, i. 294; Doc. 42). Cf. p. 53 above. Cf. the Bishop of Winchester's liberty of Taunton, the men of which in Domesday Book had to serve in the fyrd 'with the men of the bishop' (see Maitland, 197; John, 134).

[143] Doc. 65.

[144] Doc. 42.

[145] Thus Stenton, *First Century* 123–4; John, 84.

precisely that they are not fees nor (i.e. in the circumstances of the new Norman settlement) can they be converted into fees except with the Bishop's permission – 'nor [could he: *i.e.* the tenant] retain the land by usurping hereditary right [i.e. it must be given back to the church when the term of the lease is up], nor claim it as his fee, except according to the will of the bishop and according to the agreement he had made with him [the bishop]'.[146]

Both Maitland and, after him, Eric John note the distinction in Oswaldslow between royal and episcopal service but obscure its fundamental importance, for the episcopal service is non-military and the military service is royal, whereas it is of the essence of the knight's fee (and therefore of the essence of feudalism) that the holder of the fee owes military service to the lord thereof. Maitland was at least tempted to interpret the famous riding services which the lease-hold tenants owed the Bishop[147] as military, combined this in the minds of his readers with the fact that the same tenants would provide the fyrd-service due from their lands under the Bishop's banner, and allowed himself in the same passage to call the tenants 'knights'.[148] Hence, with the due proviso that 'we must not bring into undue relief the military side of the tenure',[149] he could go on to write – 'Dependent tenure is here, and, we may say, feudal tenure, and even tenure by knight's service, for though the English *cniht* of the tenth century differs much from the knight of the twelfth, still it is a change in military tactics rather than a change in legal ideas that is required to convert the one into the other'.[150] This surely is a classic instance of getting one's priorities wrong, for it is the knight and his military tactics which are fundamentals of feudalism, not the legal ideas which came later, and Maitland (for whom elsewhere 'of all the phenomena of feudalism none seems more essential than seignorial justice', compared with which 'military tenure is a superficial matter')[151] here shows himself the lawyer, divorced from reality. Eric John, on the other hand, obscures the issue chiefly by stressing an alleged 'cardinal principle' of English feudalism that 'all service is royal service'.[152] By 'all service' all military service is presumably meant, since otherwise the proposition would not stand up for a moment, and

---

[146] Doc. 65. It seems extraordinarily difficult to follow John (p. 143) in interpreting this statement to support his contention that the Oswaldslow leases are fees.

[147] They 'shall fulfil the whole law of riding as riding men should' (*ut omnes equitandi lex ab eis impleatur, que ad equites pertinet*). Doc. 42. See Maitland, 359; Stenton, 128.

[148] Maitland, 361–2.

[149] P. 362.

[150] P. 363.

[151] P. 307. Cf. above, p. 31.

[152] *Land Tenure*, 147–8.

thus amended the statement, frequently repeated by English historians, rests on Maitland's authority – 'all military service is *regale servicium*'.[153] In other words since even in post-Conquest England military service is royal, and since the military service owed by the lease-hold tenants of the bishopric of Worcester and elsewhere was royal service, there is thus no real difference between those leases and fees – to quote John again, 'It would seem, then, that estates rated in hides are not necessarily of a different kind of tenure from estates reckoned in fees'.[154] But even if the rule that all military service in post-Conquest England was the King's were true it would certainly not be of the essence of feudalism, wherein military service to the lord of the fee is central and fundamental,[155] but would have to be construed, as indeed it is generally construed, as a rule peculiar to England, derived from pre-feudal sovereignty and applied, as it were, by Anglo-Norman kings and their successors as a curb upon galloping feudalism. But was such a rule ever true of post-Conquest England, and, if so, when? All would agree that we must at once exempt from it the Marches of Wales where private warfare was a custom at least until the time of Edward I. As for England proper, such a rule accords ill with all those 'surplus knights' – knights enfeoffed and services exacted over and above what was owed to the King by the *servitia debita*, the quotas, of his tenants-in-chief, as revealed by the feudal inquest of 1166;[156] and it accords even less well with the remarkable (according to the accepted view) charter of c.1145–50 quoted by Stenton and granting exemption 'from royal as well as military services'.[157] As late as the 1180s so great an authority as the author of 'Glanville's' *Treatise on the Laws and Customs of England* could express doubt as to whether or not lords could take aids 'to maintain their own wars' – *ad guerram suam manutenendam* – and in a discussion of multiple homage, that is the case of a vassal bound to more than one lord, could envisage the problem of war between those lords. Even Maitland felt bound to comment that the latter passage 'can hardly be read otherwise than as a statement that private warfare may conceivably be lawful'.[158]

[153] F. Pollock and F. W. Maitland, *History of English Law* (Cambridge, 1895), i. 243.

[154] P. 148.

[155] Thus Maitland himself wrote: 'It might well have been otherwise; we may see that it nearly was otherwise; we may be fairly certain that in this respect the law was no adequate expression of the current morality' (*History of English Law*, i. 242–3).

[156] Cf. Stenton, *First Century*, 5.

[157] P. 184. This charter, of course, comes from the reign of Stephen, but it may well be that the alleged 'feudal anarchy' of Stephen's time is too often used as a reason to explain away awkward facts.

[158] *History of English Law*, i. 282. For the text (Glanville IX, i and viii) see the new edition of 'Glanville' by G. D. H. Hall, *The treatise on the laws and customs of the realm of England commonly called Glanville* (London, 1965), 104, 112. Doc.

In short, the lease-hold lands of Oswaldslow (or elsewhere) were not fees, nor did St Wulfstan and St Oswald think that they were, nor did William the Conqueror's Domesday commissioners think that they were, nor the men of Worcestershire who testified on oath in 1086, and by the test of our analysis they were not fees especially because they did not involve military service by the tenant to the lord as a condition of the lease. Stenton wrote that 'neither the memorandum nor the leases which it helps to interpret ever imply that the bishop has given land to a tenant in order that he may do military service'.[159] This is true of the surviving leases and the memorandum, and would be true of all the other evidence relating to the pre-Conquest bishopric of Worcester if we were to add to the end of the statement the words 'to the bishop'. For there is in Hemming's cartulary not a lease but an entry about a lease[160] which, though not cited, curiously enough, either by Maitland or by the modern critics of Round and Stenton,[161] is at first sight patient of a feudal interpretation. We are told how a certain Dane called Simund, a housecarl[162] of Earl Leofric, after the manner of his race, coveted the monks' vill of Crowle in Oswaldslow, and brought such pressure to bear, both on his own account and through his lord, that the prior of Worcester was eventually constrained to lease it to him for the term of his life (*terram ipsam concessit possidendam vite sue spatio*), 'on this condition, that he should serve the monastery for it on military expeditions by land and sea (which at that time were frequent)'. But upon reflection this is fyrd-service again. The relevant Domesday entry is to be cited at this point, for there we read that Simund had held Crowle for five hides 'and rendered to the bishop all service and geld'.[163] No one would suggest that geld was episcopal, and nor was the military service. Geld and the *trimoda necessitas*, including military service, lay upon all land including Crowle: the prior of Worcester, when against his will he leased Crowle to Simund, at least ensured that the geld and service to which it was assessed would be borne by the tenant, as he also secured recognition of his lordship over it.[164] The fyrd in which Simund was to serve, also, we are told by Hemming, as we are so often told, might go by land or sea (*expeditio terra marique* is a phrase common in Anglo-Saxon docu-

---

[159] *First Century*, 127.
[160] i. 264–5. Doc. 45.
[161] V. H. Galbraith, however, makes use of it in his 'An episcopal land-grant of 1085', *English Historical Review*, xliv. 364.
[162] *Miles* and translated by Galbraith as 'knight'.
[163] *Domesday Book*, i. 174. Doc. 68.
[164] Cf. therefore in this connection, Doc. 46.

---

64. The passage relating to aids is in Stubbs, *Select Charters*, 193. Neither passage is in the extracts printed in *English Historical Documents*, ii. For 'aid', *auxilium*, see p. 91 below.

ments), and we are thus reminded again of the point insisted upon by Eric John that the military service especially required by the King from Oswaldslow was naval service, and that its 300 hides formed a 'shipful'[165] (i.e. bound to provide the full complement of a warship, and perhaps the ship as well) – than which few things could be less feudal. In Hemming,[166] in a recorded plea between St Wulfstan and the neighbouring Abbot of Evesham touching lands and services in Oswaldslow, and again in Domesday Book,[167] we meet Edric, the steersman of the Bishop's warship and the leader of his contingent to the fyrd, and, once again, the fact that the military or naval service is royal service is explicitly stated, and the distinction between the King's service and the Bishop's is explicitly made. In Hemming it is Edric 'who in the time of King Edward was steersman (sturmannus) of the bishop's ship and leader of the forces of the same bishop to the king's service' (ad servitium regis): in Domesday Edric held five hides of the bishop in Oswaldslow, for which he provided the services 'pertaining to the king and the bishop.'

No fees, then, it would seem, in pre-Conquest Oswaldslow or England – and if no fees, no feudalism. One may also add one further point to all the others, that just as the exponents of Old English feudalism, and, more precisely, the exponents of continuity in these matters, cannot really have their fyrd evolving painlessly into the Norman feudal host, without cataclysmic change, since both fyrd and host are found together after 1066,[168] so too they cannot have their Old English leases as, or becoming, fees, since the lease also survived the Conquest to continue in the age of fees[169] – indeed in one well-known case we find in a single charter, and, as it were, side by side, land held by lease and land held by knight-service as a fief, by the same tenant of the same lord.[170] But Maitland drew attention to another point of seeming continuity, again in the context of Oswaldslow and the bishopric of Worcester, which has tended to hypnotize his successors ever since. Before the Conquest, it is alleged, Oswaldslow was obliged to send sixty men to the fyrd, and after it the quota or servitium debitum of the bishop was sixty knights. Thus Maitland – 'The Bishop of Worcester held 300 hides [i.e. Oswaldslow]

---

[165] Land Tenure, 119–21.
[166] i. 81. Doc. 46.
[167] i. 173b. Doc. 67.
[168] The evidence for the survival of the fyrd in the post-Conquest period is set out by Hollister, Military Organization of Norman England, 216ff. and 261–7. Nevertheless, while there is no doubt that the principle of the obligation of all free men to provide military service was maintained by William the Conqueror and his successors (as witness the Assize of Arms of 1181 and other subsequent enactments) one may retain some doubts as to the efficacy of the force thus raised.
[169] See Lennard, Rural England, 170ff.
[170] Galbraith, English Historical Review, xliv; Doc. 50.

over which he had sake and soke and all customs: he was bound to put 60 *milites* into the field . . . At the beginning of Henry II's reign he was charged with 60 knights' fees.[171] Maitland himself forbore from making the obvious but superficial deduction that the one is a mere continuation of the other, but Round, seeing the danger for lesser men, answered him at once.[172] He pointed out that the Worcester *servitium debitum* of sixty knights was in any case challenged by the Bishop in the twelfth century and subsequently reduced to fifty. He also pointed out, quite correctly, that there is in fact no direct evidence for the confident assertion, still frequently repeated, that the pre-Conquest contingent due from Oswaldslow was sixty men (whether 'in the field' or in the Bishop's ship): it was simply assumed by Maitland by the application of the five-hide rule for fyrd-service (300 divided by 5 = 60), to which assumption Eric John has more recently added the somewhat flimsy and imprecise supporting evidence that the normal size of an Anglo-Saxon warship was 'approximately sixty oars'.[173] But Round's main point was obvious and, surely, unanswerable. Maitland's sixty men for the pre-Conquest fyrd were from Oswaldslow, which we know to have been assessed at 300 hides from Domesday Book,[174] while the post-Conquest quota of sixty knights was imposed upon the whole bishopric (reckoned by Round at between 500 and 600 hides), of which Oswaldslow was only a part. The part cannot possibly be identified with the whole, nor is this huge objection met by Miss Hollings' abstruse calculations, designed to bring the hidation of the whole bishopric down to c.300 hides by the very dubious expedient of exempting demesne land from military service, even if they could be accepted, which, it seems, they cannot.[175] In short, one cannot, even at Worcester, find any connection, any continuity, between the pre-Conquest assessment for military service in the fyrd (whether it went by land or sea) and the quotas, the *servitia debita*, of knight-service demanded from the same lands after 1066.[176]

At this point, of course, we meet with Round's great thesis, no longer unchallenged but still unbroken. In his seminal paper, 'The Introduction of Knight-Service into England',[177] Round was able to establish from later twelfth-century evidence, notably the *Carte Baronum* of

[171] *Domesday Book and Beyond*, 199.

[172] 'Military Tenure before the Conquest,' *English Historical Review*, xii (1897).

[173] *Land Tenure*, 121. 'Approximately' seems scarcely good enough for the mathematical approach to history. A good note on the subject will be found in C. Plummer, *Two of the Saxon Chronicles Parallel* (Oxford, 1892-9), ii. 185-6. Cf. Hollister, *Anglo-Saxon Military Institutions*, 108-12.

[174] i. 172*b*. Doc. 66.

[175] 'The survival of the five-hide unit in the Western Midlands,' *English Historical Review*, lxiii. 457-60. Cf. Hollister, *Anglo-Saxon Military Institutions*, 53-5; Darlington, *Norman Conquest*, 25, n. 4.

[176] Not even Eric John can do it. See *Land Tenure*, p. 158; cf. p. 64 below.

[177] Printed in his *Feudal England*: see p. 19 n. 9 above.

1166[178] and the Pipe Rolls,[179] the *servitia debita* or quotas of knight-service known to have been demanded by post-Conquest kings from their tenants-in-chief both lay and ecclesiastical, and then to trace these quotas back to the reign of William the Conqueror but no further. He was able to deduce, partly from other ancillary evidence yet to be discussed,[180] but notably from the rough, round numbers of the quotas (frequently divisible by five and ten) and their failure to bear any relation either to the pre-Conquest assessment of the same lands or even to their value, that they were in fact the product of the Conqueror's arbitrary will, a series of *ad hoc* bargains and arrangements with his individual vassals. Thus Round's conclusion as relevant now as when he first drew it against the exponents of continuity in his own day: 'As against the theory that the military obligation of the Anglo-Norman tenant-in-chief was determined by the assessment of his holding, whether in hidage or in value, I maintain that the extent of that obligation was not determined by his holding, but was fixed in relation to, and expressed in terms of, the *constabularia* of ten knights, the unit of the feudal host. And I, consequently, hold that his military service was in no way derived or developed from that of the Anglo-Saxons, but was arbitrarily fixed by the King, from whom he received his fief, irrespectively both of its size and of all pre-existing arrangements'.[181] Stenton, writing forty years on, observed that all subsequent work had 'confirmed Round's main position that the amount of knight service which King William demanded from his several tenants-in-chief bore no definite relation to the extent or value of their lands',[182] and himself concluded that 'Within a generation after the battle [of Hastings], the Norman conquerors had established in central and southern England, and introduced into the region beyond Humber, a system of military service which at every point ignored Old English precedent'.[183]

A moment's consideration of the sheer arbitrariness of the quotas, in some cases, as with the disproportionately heavy burden placed upon Peterborough Abbey, evidently reflecting known political factors of the Conqueror's day,[184] is almost alone sufficient to convince one of the inherent probability of Round's position and of the conventional view that the quotas of feudal knight-service were established by King William

[178] Printed in *The Red Book of the Exchequer*, ed. Hubert Hall (Rolls Series, London, 1896), i. 186–445.
[179] See the publications of The Pipe Roll Society.
[180] Notably the Evesham Writ of 1072 (below and Doc. 47) and the chronicle evidence (discussed p. 87 below.)
[181] *Feudal England*, 261.
[182] *First Century*, 122.
[183] Ibid., 121.
[184] H. M. Chew, *English Ecclesiastical Tenants-in-Chief and Knight Service* (London, 1932), 7–8.

as part and parcel of the Norman settlement, while the now famous writ of the Conqueror to Æthelwig Abbot of Evesham, together with other evidence, shows they were early established. That writ, first published by Round 'as a climax to my argument', to be dated certainly before 1077 and almost certainly to 1072, summons the Abbot to be before the King with 'those five knights which you owe me in respect of your abbacy', five knights being the known quota of Evesham from later twelfth-century evidence.[185] It may be that Round lost a trick by insisting upon the Norman *constabularia* of ten (though in fact the evidence for that is at least better than his critics will allow)[186] as 'the unit of the feudal host' in place of the Anglo-Saxon five-hide unit, for it was sufficient for his purposes, as it is for ours, to show the origins of English feudalism by accumulating the overwhelming evidence for the imposition of the quotas of knight-service by the Conqueror's arbitrary will, without reference to any previous assessment. Eric John may make the point that Round in pushing the quotas back to the Conqueror's reign could not scientifically establish a *terminus a quo*,[187] but it does seem that he established a *ne plus ultra*, for no one has been able to push them back further, and no one, not even Eric John, not even for Worcester,[188] has been able to show any connection between them and any previous and pre-Conquest assessment of the same lands to military service (which was in any case of a different kind). And as J. O. Prestwich observed, 'If the case for continuity will not work in Worcestershire it is weak indeed' – the point being that the estates of the Church alone had an institutional continuity at the time of the Conquest in that they could be neither broken up nor redistributed, while Worcester in the event was unique in the survival of its pre-Conquest English bishop, St Wulfstan, throughout the Conqueror's regin and well into the reign of Rufus.

At a lower level than the large quotas of the great tenants-in-chief, however, there is an occasional element of continuity to which much, and too much, attention has been paid, namely the occasional 'survival of the

---

[185] For the writ, see Round, 304 (with commentary, 303–5); Stubbs, *Select Charters*, 97; *English Historical Documents*, ii. 895; Doc. 47. The occasion is almost certainly the summons of the feudal host for the Scottish expedition of 1072. The text of the writ falls into two parts: in the first, the abbot as a local official is to summon 'all those who are under your administration and jurisdiction' to have before the King at Clarendon on the Octaves of Whitsun all the knights which they owe; in the second, the Abbot himself is to come with the five knights owed from his abbey. For other evidence of the early imposition of the quotas after the Conquest, and of the subsequent process of subinfeudation by the tenants-in-chief, see Round, 295–308, and below, pp. 86ff.

[186] Round, 259–60. Cf. Hollister, *Military Organization of Norman England*, 32–4; Galbraith, *English Historical Review*, xliv. 370–1.

[187] *Land Tenure*, 150.

[188] Ibid., 158. Cf. Prestwich, *Past and Present*, No. 26, p. 44, quoted below.

five-hide unit' of pre-Conquest days into the post-Conquest period in the form of fees rated at five hides, or, it may be, small multiples thereof, or, in the case of fractional fees (fees owing less than a whole knight's service), fractions thereof. In itself the phenomenon need not surprise us, nor, certainly, be held of sufficient importance to make us question the view that feudalism is a Norman importation and its military system of knight-service unrelated to the military system of the fyrd. Once again we must remember that the latter produced infantry-men or naval forces, and the former produced knights.[189] For the rest, it is only reasonable to expect that Norman institutions, however new and alien to England, would here and there be to some extent bent or effected by pre-existing English customs, just as so many Old English institutions survived the Conquest (including the fyrd) though bent and altered by the Normans. Especially is this so since the Norman and French settlers after 1066 were only a small proportion of the population,[190] and, moreover, since sociologically the Norman settlement was pre-eminently the establishment of a new ruling class and aristocracy upon the land, we might expect, what indeed we find, that Old English custom is more in evidence the nearer to the grass roots of society we get. Round rightly taught us to make a useful mental distinction between the initial imposition of the quotas by William the Conqueror upon his great tenants-in-chief, and the secondary and subsequent process of 'subinfeudation' wherein those magnates in turn enfeoffed their own knights and vassals. Both processes were alike a series of individual, *ad hoc* and arbitrary bargains between lord and tenant-to-be, with no necessary connection with any preceding tenures and arrangements, but at the lower end of the process of subinfeudation, at the level, for example, of the simple knight with no knight-vassals of his own, we get close to the grass roots, and what more likely, for example, than that the estate of some dispossessed thegn or housecarl or prosperous ceorl, rated at five hides under the old dispensation, should be handed over intact and without addition to the newcomer as a fief?

Round himself, who was at least as aware of the prevalence of the five-hide and six-carucate unit in pre-Conquest England as any of the more recent writers on the subject, was also aware of its survival in the form of five-hide fees.[191] He attributed the circumstance as 'merely, I think, due

---

[189] The Serjeanty tenures of post-Conquest England (for which see E. A. Kimball, *Serjeanty Tenure in Medieval England*, New Haven, 1936), which produced either military service of a lower grade than knight-service or miscellaneous, and sometimes picturesque, services of a non-military and miscellaneous nature, are relatively few in number and are best regarded as the result of the overflow of feudal concepts into spheres other than military or knightly.

[190] Perhaps ten thousand in a total population of one and a half million. See H. R. Loyn, *The Norman Conquest* (London, 1965), 119; Brown, *Normans*, 211.

[191] *Feudal England*, 44ff, 293.

to the existence of five-hide estates, survivals from the previous *régime*', and quite rightly did not allow it to affect his main position since he went on to demonstrate that, in general 'no fixed number of hides constituted a knight's fee' which could and did, if we survey all the evidence for England as a whole, vary almost indefinitely in its hidation.[192] A fee consisting of five hides, or a multiple or fraction thereof, is just one more variant in an endless series of variations, and there is no sign of any regular or uniform connection between the knight's fee and the previous assessment of the same land for military services, any more than there is between the great fiefs or honors of the tenants-in-chief with their quotas of knights and the previous assessment of their lands. Both were new – as indeed to contemporaries both were the same thing, the honor being the great fief of a great man. Any amount of land held by a vassal of a lord in return for any amount of knight-service is a fee, and indeed, as Stenton pointed out, the concept of 'the knight's fee', the *feudum unius militis*, as a unit of land supporting one knight, and thus a unit of calculation for administrators, was slow to develop, which fact alone may be regarded as 'conclusive evidence against any theory that knight-service in England was originally based on territorial units of uniform, or even approximately uniform standard'.[193]

It might have been better had matters been left so, but unfortunately they have not been. Some years ago Miss Marjory Hollings, in an article entitled, 'The Survival of the Five-Hide Unit in the Western Midlands', claimed to have discovered in the Red Book of Worcester, which she edited and which was unknown to Round, new evidence to prove that on the post-Conquest bishopric of Worcester (Worcester again) fees regularly consisted of five hides or were based upon the five-hide unit and were deliberately constructed so to do.[194] Miss Hollings was of the opinion that had Round known of her new evidence 'it is more than probable that he would have modified his theory of knight service', but it is difficult to see why the master (who was well aware of five-hide fees at Worcester among other places) should have amended his thesis one iota.[195] Even if Miss Hollings' contention were true, the proper response of the intelligent student should be simply 'So what?', for we are left with the infinite variety of fees everywhere else,

---

[192] Pp. 293-5.

[193] *First Century*, 157.

[194] *English Historical Review*, lxiii (1948). An abbreviated version of this monograph is included in her Introduction to her *Red Book of Worcester*, edited for the Worcestershire Historical Society, vol. iv, 1950, pp. xxff. In what follows reference is made to the fuller version except where otherwise noted.

[195] Hollings, 454. Cf. Round, *Feudal England*, 293-4. It is, indeed, more than probable that had Round seen the work of Miss Hollings he would have blown the author out of the water in his customary fashion.

and if it had pleased the conservative Bishop of Worcester[196] and his officials to make up their new fees in terms of the five-hide unit it would be an interesting exercise in antiquarianism but still no more than one more variation in a world of heterogeneous fees.[197] But is Miss Hollings' contention, which appears to be widely accepted, in fact sound and sustained by the evidence upon which it is based? It should be said at once that more work needs to be done upon the material in question, which consists of lists of fees and notes upon fees towards the end of the Red Book of Worcester, for Miss Hollings' edition of the text leaves much to be desired and her commentary upon it is at times so difficult to follow as to be incomprehensible. It is also to be noted that in using the Red Book we are more stages than usual removed from the facts recorded in it, for the original manuscript is lost and we are in practice using (the printed edition of) an eighteenth-century transcript of a late thirteenth-century compilation, which itself, of course, comprised transcripts of the earlier material we seek.

That said, Miss Hollings' main piece of evidence for the regular and systematic preservation of the five-hide unit by the bishopric of Worcester in the make-up of its fees is the now famous memorandum or note, 'Memorandum that 4 virgates of land make one hide and 5 hides make 1 knight's fee' (*Memorandum quod iiij virgate terre faciunt j hidam et quinque hide faciunt j feudum militis*).[198] The first point to note is that, in the original manuscript (now lost), above the word 'five' [hides], 'four' had been written in a later or different hand – which may un-nerve those who feel that mathematical equations must be based upon numerical precision. The next point to note is the immediate context and circumstance of the note or memorandum, which is an insertion of *c*.1298 in a list of the bishop's fees originally drawn up in 1208–9 but copied out in 1298 and subsequently inserted in the Red Book.[199] We are, therefore, long centuries away from the original enfeoffments made in the bishopric after the Conquest. Moreover, while in this list some of the tenants of the Bishop's desmesne holding fractional fees – i.e. small parcels of land owing less than the service of a whole knight – have their service assessed in terms of the five-hide system (e.g. *x* holds 'one hide by the service of

---

[196] I.e. Wulfstan (II, 1062–95) since most of the enfeoffments were early (cf. Hollings, 463).

[197] Cf. Darlington, *Norman Conquest*, 24.

[198] *Red Book*, 445. Doc. 74 (p. 155).

[199] Another memorandum at the end of the list (Doc. 74; *Red Book*, 449) states that it was sought and found in the Royal Treasury at Westminster by Alfred de Northgrave in May 1298. The same list (without, of course, the memoranda) is printed in the *Book of Fees*, where it is dated (by the editors) 1208–9, the original occasion of its compilation being the seizure of the bishopric by King John after the Papal interdict (*Book of Fees*, London, H. M. Stationery Office, Pt. i, 1920, 34 and 35–9).

the fifth part of a knight', and the like – Doc. 74), the memorandum itself is inserted by the Worcester scribe at the end of the analysis of the large fee of the Bishop's substantial mesne-tenant, William de Beauchamp, who owed the service of fifteen knights, but many of whose own under-tenants are there listed as holding only small parcels of land, set down in terms of hides and virgates. To these the memorandum is directly relevant, but there is no warrant to read into it a golden rule for the constitution of fees throughout the bishopric of Worcester in all periods including the early period of the original enfeoffments. Its most natural interpretation would be as an administrator's rule of thumb, used in the thirteenth century and no doubt earlier, especially for the just apportionment, upon small estates held by knight-service, of scutages, aids and reliefs, or any other feudal 'incidents' raised in cash at the rate of so much per fee. That this is what in fact it was is sufficiently shown by the list of a scutage taken in the reign of Edward I which immediately follows the 1208–9 list of fees, and which also explains the seeming discrepancy of five or four hides to the fee in the memorandum.[200] That scutage was assessed at 40s to the fee,[201] but of those who owe scutage but hold only a fraction of a fee expressed simply in hides and virgates, some pay at the rate of five hides to the fee[202] and some (in fact more) pay at the rate of four.[203] Supplied with this knowledge and this key, we can then also understand why in preceding lists of fees and notes about fees entered in the Red Book the compiler went out of his way to note, *where appropriate*, that the tenant 'answered' or 'served' at the rate of five hides to the fee. Thus, for example, 'Philip de Haster holds Deyleford of the bishop and answers to the bishop concerning knight-service (*de militia*) as much as pertains to three hides where five hides make one knight,'[204] or 'Walter de Haya holds two geldable hides by service whereof five hides make a knight.'[205]

It will be observed that none of this so far has anything necessarily to do with the original make-up of the Worcester fees, the original enfeoffments and sub-infeudations or, in Miss Hollings' words, 'the principle on which the fee is to be constructed'.[206] On the contrary, it could be

---

[200] *Red Book*, 449–51.

[201] Thus e.g., 449, *De domino W. Corbet pro j feodo militis xls; De domino Radulfo de Wilintone pro dimidio feodo xxs.*

[202] E.g. 450, *De Willelmo Mansel pro una hida viiis.*

[203] E.g. 450, *De Willelmo Savage et Roberto le Botiler pro una hida x s.; De Ricardo de Grenville pro dimidia hida in Helmintone v s.*

[204] *Philippus de Haster tenet de Episcopo Deyleford et respondit Episcopo de militia quantum ad iij hidas pertinet, ubi v hidas [sic] faciunt j militem,* 435.

[205] *Walterus de Haya tenet ij hidas geldabiles per servitium unde quinque hide faciunt militem,* 436.

[206] *English Historical Review*, lxiii. 455.

that later administrators of the Bishop's lands, faced with the *fait accompli* of numerous small estates of various sizes, are seeking to make some sense of them. The same bureaucratic process of tidying up a situation originally untidy presumably also lies behind the long series of notes, dated by Miss Hollings to the later twelfth century, wherein numerous fragmentary holdings are bundled into various combinations to make a whole fee.[207] The object of the exercise would seem to be to make viable units for actual service (services being obviously less easily divisible than the money payments for which they were therefore often commuted), as for example in the list of 'Riding Knights' (*Milites Equitantes*) for escort services entered hereabouts,[208] and the result is sometimes an (artificial) fee of five hides and sometimes not. And where the Red Book of Worcester does show the actual make-up of actual fees, large or small, i.e. the 'honor' of a substantial tenant of the Bishop, or the single knight's fee of a knight, or a fragment of a knight's fee expressed as such (half a fee, or a quarter), and presumably as they were in the beginning when first created, these too, *pace* Miss Hollings, are sometimes made up of five hides, or multiples, or divisions thereof, but just as often not. Thus the earliest list of knights' fees in the Red Book of Worcester is quite clearly the Bishop's version or draft of his return to the Feudal Inquest of 1166 and is entered accordingly, more or less verbatim, in the Red Book of the Exchequer.[209] It contains only the large fiefs or whole knights' fees or substantial fractions of knights' fees, and in general makes no reference to the small estates of hides and virgates which we have so far been discussing. But at one point, for the

---

[207] *Red Book*, 413–16, 430–42. They are dated to the later twelfth century and the time of Bishop Roger of Gloucester by Miss Hollings, *English Historical Review*, lxiii. 454. There is no warranty for her further statement, *Red Book*, 413, n. 6, that they were 'intended to show how the bishop's quota was made up, in support of his claim that he had been assessed at more than his due service'. For the claim that the Worcester quota was fifty, not sixty, knights, see p. 62 above and Hollings, *English Historical Review*, lxiii. 454.

[208] *Red Book*, 416–18.

[209] *Red Book of Worcester*, iv. 412–13. Cf. *Red Book of the Exchequer*, ed. Hall, i. 300–1; Doc. 72, where the two are collated. It is not clear why Miss Hollings refers enigmatically to this list as 'the earliest list(s) extant', only occasionally and, as it were, reluctantly relating it to the inquest of 1166 (see *English Historical Review*, lxiii. 453, 454; *Red Book of Worcester*, i, pp. iv–v; iv, pp. xx, xxi and n. 1 to p. 412 where the list is printed). The clue may be that in her article the suggestion is made that at Worcester the 'old enfeoffment' is pre-Conquest (481–3). In fact the oldest extant list of the Bishop's knights is presumably that contained in Rufus' writ of 1095, printed in full by Round, *Feudal England*, 309 (Doc. 51 and below). Though Round was able to identify many of the tenants with their holdings in Domesday Book, they do not appear to relate at all easily to the knight-tenants of the old enfeoffment in 1166. It should certainly be noted that the reliefs demanded by Rufus seem entirely arbitrary, unrelated either to the hidage or knight-service of the lands where known.

enfeoffments of Bishop Samson's time (1096–1112), it takes us behind the bare list of the Exchequer version to show the actual make-up of the fees in hides and virgates.[210] In only one of the five instances (as it happens, the one cited by Miss Hollings)[211] do five hides make one knight. Frederick de Bissopesdone owes the service of one knight in return for five hides, but of the others Adam de Crombe owes one knight in return for seven and a quarter hides, Sampson de Salcemarisco owes the service of half a knight in return for five and a half hides, Illi de Turri holds five and three-quarter hides for one knight, and Jordan Destone three and a quarter for half a knight.

If we go further back yet towards the beginning, beyond the lists of the Red Book of Worcester or the Bishop's return of 1166, to the early list of episcopal tenants contained in Rufus' writ demanding reliefs in 1095 (not noticed by Miss Hollings) and make use of Round's analysis of the holdings of those tenants in terms of hides from Domesday Book, we again see little trace of any five-hide principle.[212] As for the Red Book of Worcester itself, there are very many instances indeed where such a principle does not apply, to set against those where it does, including, as merely one example, three hides held by the King himself 'for a fee of two knights'.[213] It may be also that, as Miss Hollings states, 'the same principle [*i.e.* of five hides to the fee] is noticeable' in the great fiefs which Bohun and Beauchamp held of the Bishop,[214] but if so the principle is more honoured in the breach than in the observance. In practice Bohun held thirty-seven hides for the service of four knights, although admittedly the Bishop claimed a further three-and-a-half knights at least as early as 1166.[215] In the case of Beauchamp, who held one hundred and nine-and-a-half hides for the service of fifteen knights, no comment is made in the 1166 list of fees, and it is only in the slightly later list of *c.*1164–79 that, as Miss Hollings in a rather unguarded moment put it, the 'discovery' of the discrepancy was made, and the hopeful note added to a survey of the Beauchamp fee in the Red Book of Worcester: 'All these [hides] he says he holds of the Bishop for a fee of 15 knights where there should be a fee of twenty-two knights at least except for half a hide'. The 'at least' lacks mathematical precision and, further yet, the 1208–9 list of fees in the Red Book of Worcester, containing with reference to Beauchamp the famous memorandum already quoted, claims that he owes not twenty-two knights but twenty-five and

---

[210] *Red Book of Worcester*, iv, 412–13; Doc. 72.
[211] *English Historical Review*, lxiii. 455.
[212] Doc. 51; Round, *Feudal England*, 312. Round was able to identify in Domesday the tenures of fifteen of the tenants named in the writ. In only five cases is their total hidage obviously divisible by five.
[213] iv. 432; Doc. 73.
[214] *English Historical Review*, lxiii, 455.
[215] *Red Book of Worcester*, iv. 412, 438. Doc. 72.

a half – a claim bearing no relation to any five-hide rule.[216] Not even, therefore, in the bishopric of Worcester did five hides regularly make a knight's fee, and even in the bishopric of Worcester fees varied widely in their hidation.

There is, before we leave it, one more point to be made in connection with the fee and, more particularly, in connection with the attempt to equate the lease-hold tenures of the pre-Conquest bishopric of Worcester with post-Conquest fees. Stenton, in rightly insisting that this cannot be done, several times emphasizes as an essential difference the lack of any precise definition of service in the leases themselves, or even in St Oswald's memorandum, as opposed to the precision in this matter of eleventh- and twelfth-century charters of enfeoffment. 'The services for which Oswald stipulated were miscellaneous and he left their exact nature vague. There is no trace in his memorandum of the feudal ideas that the services to be rendered for a tenement should admit of a close definition, and that if more than a single form of service is required from the same holding, the services with which it is associated should be of a cognate character'.[217] Again, 'the difference between the indefiniteness of Oswald's leases, and the precision of the twelfth-century charter of enfeoffment, represents a difference between the habits of thought of two races'.[218] The thesis being developed here is an elaboration of and deduction from the more valid distinction which Stenton makes elsewhere between late Old English society wherein a man's status depended upon law (his *wergild* or blood-price) and inheritance, and early feudal society wherein status was more immediately functional, dependent upon the type of service rendered, with the social palm going to the specialized knight.[219] The knight and his specialized service we have indeed seen to be a fundamental of feudalism, but to follow Stenton further and to insist that 'there is a fundamental difference between a statement that a tenant must fulfil the whole law of riding' [*i.e.* in Oswald's memorandum] 'and a statement that he must ride with his lord or his lord's wife from Baseford to Ashby Magna' [*i.e.* in a twelfth-century charter duly cited],[220] is to take a step which the post-Conquest documentary evidence itself will not support. Beyond specifying

---

[216] *Red Book of Worcester*, iv. 412, 434; Docs. 72–3. *English Historical Review*, lxiii. 460. Cf. however the 1208–9 list of fees where, in the *Red Book of Worcester*, 444 (Doc. 74) it is stated that William de Beauchamp serves for fifteen and a half knights but denies a further ten fees (*et decem feoda dedit* – a remark not found in the official royal list in the *Book of Fees*, 35) – i.e. here the episcopal claim is for 25½ Beauchamp fees. Once again one notes that this is very treacherous ground upon which to deploy the mathematical approach to feudalism.

[217] *First Century*, 124.

[218] Ibid., 123 *n*. 2.

[219] Pp. 5, 129–30.

[220] P. 129.

knight-service, the earliest charters of enfeoffment are notoriously lacking in any detailed definition of the service required,[221] and a principal theme of English feudalism and of English constitutional history alike, from the time of the Conqueror to the time of Edward I and beyond, with Magna Carta as a milestone upon the way, is the gradual definition of obligation, the slow working-out, not, it is true, of what is owed, but of how much and when. By an over-insistence, therefore, upon the definition of service as itself a mark of feudalism, Stenton lays himself open to the charge, duly made for example by Miss Hollings (though the point as usual had first been made by Maitland)[222] that 'if a close definition of services is essential to feudalism, the establishment of feudalism in England can hardly be dated much earlier than the reign of Henry II'.[223]

4. *Absence of native castles*
From the fief we turn to the fourth and last of the fundamentals of feudalism, namely the castle, to be defined as the fortified residence of a lord. It is a remarkable fact that the history of the castle in England (and in Wales, in Scotland and in Ireland) was only first worked out and established at the beginning of this present century, before which confusion and loose thinking reigned supreme, with Saxon castles and Roman castles and Ancient British castles, some of which (e.g. Maiden's 'Castle') are still enshrined among our place-names and upon our maps. The scholar chiefly responsible for the advance was Mrs E. S. Armitage, wife of a Yorkshire clergyman, whose seminal work, published in its final form in 1912,[224] first traced the origin of the castle on the Continent, setting it in its proper context as an integral part of feudal society, and then went on to show beyond all reasonable doubt that the castle in this country was a French and Norman importation, the result of the Norman Conquest. So matters stood until literally now, when, amongst archaeologists rather than historians (and unfortunately the regrettable distinction still has to be made), interest in the origin of the English castle has been revived in the last few years, and, in consequence, the question of the presence or absence of the castle in pre-Conquest England once

[221] Docs. 48–50.
[222] *Domesday Book and Beyond*, 361 – 'As to the services to be rendered [i.e. in Oswald's Memorandum], if we compare them with those of which Glanville and Bracton speak, they will seem both miscellaneous and indefinite; perhaps we ought to say that they are all the more feudal on that account.' Upon which, cf. Stenton, 123 *n.* 2.
[223] *English Historical Review*, lxiii, 472–3.
[224] *Early Norman Castles of the British Isles*, London, 1912. Behind this lies a monograph on English castles, *English Historical Review*, xix (1904), and one on Irish, *Antiquary*, xlii (1906).

more raised.[225] The case, therefore, must once more be rehearsed, though we may notice again that the question itself is an old one, Mrs Armitage having been in her day stimulated in research and provoked into print by the insistence of her predecessor in the field, G. T. 'Castle' Clark, upon Anglo-Saxon castles.[226]

To prove a negative is always difficult because one is bound to depend in large part upon negative evidence, with all its hazards, not least in this period when positive evidence is not abundant. Nevertheless, in this case the negative evidence alone may seem conclusive, as Mrs Armitage pointed out.[227] Save for the few exceptional instances to be discussed in a moment, we simply do not hear of castles, nor meet the word, in pre-Conquest England, in the chronicles or in the laws, in the writs or in the charters. To cite one particularly telling moment in this sustained silence, it is inconceivable that, had King Edward, Earl Godwin and the other English magnates possessed castles, or been accustomed to the concept of private fortification like their opposite numbers in Normandy and France, we should not hear of it in the chronicles at the time of the political crisis and rebellion of 1051–2,[228] as the contemporary Norman chroniclers refer at once to the raising and fortification of castles in the crises of 1035 and 1047, and to the demolition of castles by the victorious Duke William thereafter.[224] By contrast the English sources for 1051–2 refer only to the castles of the 'Frenchmen', i.e. Edward's so-called Norman favourites,[230] who, with all they stood for, were themselves a principal cause of the trouble. We may begin also to introduce a more positive type of evidence, as it were, to fill the vacuum. Thus castles, the private fortresses and fortified residences of lords, like other good things, appear to have spread through feudal society at this time from the top, the prince, downwards;[231] yet where the site of a pre-Conquest English royal residence is known and has been investigated, at Cheddar or at King Edward's Westminster, no fortification is apparent – Westminster, for example, thus standing in sharp contrast to the fortified palace, the castle, of the Norman dukes at Rouen, whose great tower or *donjon*

[225] See B. K. Davison, 'The Origins of the Castle in England,' *Archaeological Journal*, cxxiv (1967). Cf. R. Allen Brown, 'An Historian's Approach to the Origins of the Castle in England,' *Arch. Journ.* cxxvi (1969).

[226] His *magnum opus*, incorporating many scattered articles, and still with its uses, is *Mediaeval Military Architecture in England* (2 vols., London, 1884).

[227] *Early Norman Castles*, 11.

[228] Cf. Armitage, 22. For the occasion, see e.g. Brown, *Normans*, 119ff.

[229] E.g. William of Jumièges, *Gesta Normannorum Ducum*, ed. J. Marx (Paris and Rouen, 1914), 115–6, 123; William of Poitiers, *Histoire de Guillaume le Conquérant*, ed. R. Foreville (Paris, 1962), 14–16, 18, 20. Docs. 21, 22, 24.

[230] See below.

[231] *Arch. Journ.*, cxxvi. 141; J. Yver, 'Les châteaux-forts en Normandie . . .', *Bulletin de la Société des Antiquaires de Normandie*, liii (1957). Cf. Armitage, 28.

dated back to the tenth century and the time of Duke Richard I.[232] Moreover, all that we know of the Old English defensive system shows it to have been, right down to 1066, like the overall military organization of which it formed a part, national as opposed to feudal, consisting of a network of royal burghs, large, public and communal fortifications, built like Ethelfleda's burgh of Worcester 'to shelter all the folk',[233] first planted by Alfred and his successors in the wars against the Danes, and in many cases still, in 1066, viable fortresses, fortified towns. It was to these and other fortified towns and cities that the invading Norman armies in 1066 moved rapidly before and after Hastings, and there often enough – as seemingly at Hastings itself, and Pevensey, Dover and London – and almost, one might say, for the convenience of students, planted within the larger, pre-existing enclosure that smaller, and thus contrasting, castle which their society and military organization alike required.[234] There is also in this matter the positive statement of Ordericus Vitalis, writing, it is true, in the next generation, but the chronicler above all others who, by the depth of his detail and interest, opens the door and lifts the veil upon the feudal society of the late eleventh and early twelfth centuries. According to Orderic, the paucity of castles in England in 1066 was one reason for the success of the Norman Conquest – 'For the fortresses which the Gauls call castles [*castella*] had been very few in the English provinces and for this reason the English, although warlike and courageous, had nevertheless shown themselves too weak to withstand their enemies'.[235]

It is to be noted, for what it is worth, that Orderic does not say there were no castles at all in England before the Conquest, and we must certainly take note at this point of those few exceptional instances of castles known to have been founded before 1066, because they are exceptions of the best sort, exceptions which prove the rule, viz. that the castle in England is a Norman and French importation. For in each case the founder of the castle concerned is a French or Breton lord already here, i.e. one of the 'Norman favourites' of Edward the Confessor.[236] Speaking of the flight of these 'Frenchmen' from London in

---

[232] For Westminster, see W. R. Lethaby in *Archaeologia*, lx (1906). For Cheddar, P. Rahtz in *Medieval Archaeology*, vi–vii (1962–3). For Rouen, see Brown in *The Bayeux Tapestry*, ed. Stenton (2nd. edition, London, 1965), p. 81 and the sources there cited.

[233] *Cartularium Saxonicum*, ed. W. de G. Birch, ii. 222. Cf. Armitage, 21.

[234] *Arch. Journ.*, cxxvi. 140. For Dover, see below. For London, see B. K. Davison in *Château-Gaillard* ii, *Kolloquium Büderich bei Düsseldorf* (Köln, 1967) 40–3. For Hastings see A. J. Taylor, in *Château-Gaillard* iii, *Conference at Battle, Sussex* (London, 1969), 144ff.

[235] *Ecclesiastical History*, ed. Chibnall, ii. 218. Doc. 31.

[236] For what follows, see Round, *Feudal England*, 317ff: Armitage, 23–5; and for the most recent discussion, Brown, *Normans*, 114–7, and in *Château-Gaillard*, iii, 'The Norman Conquest and the Genesis of English Castles'.

1052, when Earl Godwin returned in arms from his brief banishment, the 'E' version of the Anglo-Saxon Chronicle states that 'they took horses and departed, some west to Pentecost's castle, and some north to Robert's castle'.[237] Round identified with some probability 'Pentecost's castle' as Ewyas Harold, the castle of Osbern Pentecost in Herefordshire, and 'Robert's castle' as the castle of Robert fitz Wimarc at Clavering in Essex.[238] In Herefordshire there were evidently at least three other castles, in addition to Ewyas Harold, pertaining to the Norman colony planted there by King Edward under the leadership of his nephew Ralph, the son of his sister, Godgifu, who had married Drogo, Count of the Vexin. Thus, writing of the events of 1052 and the banishment of many of those whom he specifically calls Normans on Godwin's return, Florence of Worcester says that Osbern Pentecost and his associate (*socius*), Hugh, surrendered their castles (*castella*, in the plural) and went to Scotland,[239] alluding therefore to at least one other castle, unnamed and belonging to Hugh. Richard's Castle in Herefordshire is also a strong claimant to pre-Conquest foundation, its lord, Richard son of Scrob, being already established in the district in 1052 and allowed to remain by the Godwin faction in that year.[240] It seems extremely probable also that Earl Ralph, who was made Earl of Hereford in 1053 if not before, himself had a castle at Hereford, probably as early as 1051, though the actual date of its foundation is unknown.[241]

Clavering, then, in Essex, with Ewyas Harold, Richard's Castle, Hereford and at least one other site in Herefordshire, these and these alone are the only known or probable pre-Conquest English castles, and all pertain to the 'Norman favourites' of Edward the Confessor. It has often been pointed out also, by Mrs Armitage amongst others,[242] how references to these castles (the vernacular word, in the singular, is *castel, castele, castelle*) in the Anglo-Saxon Chronicle seem to indicate with a disapproving note their unpopular and alien novelty – 'the foreigners then had built a castle in Herefordshire in earl Swein's province, and had inflicted every possible injury and insult upon the king's men in those parts'.[243] It is not, however, exclusively true, as Mrs

[237] Ed. D. Whitelock, 125; Doc. 7.
[238] *Feudal England*, 324; *Victoria County Histories, Essex*, i. 345.
[239] Ed. Thorpe, i. 210; Doc. 16.
[240] Florence of Worcester, i. 210; Brown, *Normans*, 116–7. Cf. Stenton, *Anglo-Saxon England*, 554, n. 1.
[241] Brown, *Normans*, 116–7. *Pace* Stenton, as above p. 554, n. 1, Hereford castle is not mentioned in the Anglo-Saxon Chronicle for 1055, which reads ('C') 'And earl Harold had a ditch made about the *town*, during that time', the vernacular word used being *port* (ed. Whitelock, 131; cf. C. Plummer, *Two of the Saxon Chronicles Parallel*, i. 186).
[242] Armitage, 23–4. Cf. Freeman, *Norman Conquest*, ii (1870), 137 ('Both the name and the thing were new').
[243] 'E', 1051, ed. Whitelock, 119. Doc. 6.

Armitage maintained, that 'it is in connection with these Norman favourites that the word *castel* appears for the first time in the Anglo-Saxon Chronicle',[244] for Dover is also referred to as *castelle* in 1051 – as indeed Latin chronicles both on the English and the Norman side refer to it as *castrum* and *castellum* in 1051, 1064 and 1066.[245] For 1051, the 'D' version of the Anglo-Saxon Chronicle tells us that Earl Godwin and his sons threatened the King with war 'unless Eustace [count of Boulogne] were surrendered and his men handed over to them, as well as the Frenchmen who were in the castle [*castelle*].'[246] The whole context of this passage indicates that the unnamed castle is Dover, and not somewhere in Herefordshire which is its usual interpretation,[247] while Florence of Worcester specifically identifies it as Dover (*castellum in Doruverniae clivo*) in his Latin text closely based upon 'D'.[248] However, in the 'E' version of the Anglo-Saxon Chronicle for the same year 1051, Dover is *burge* and *burh*,[249] and there is much evidence to suggest that the fortress in question in 1051, 1064 and 1066 was in fact the large, communal enclosure of the former Iron Age defences[250] up on the cliff, then serving as an Old English borough (as the surviving late Saxon church of St Mary-in-Castro within it still indicates), and that this was the *castrum* or *castellum* of Harold's oath in 1064,[251] which the victorious duke William hastened to take and occupy after Hastings in 1066, then planting his castle inside it.[252] Such an hypothesis also, which has lately received a measure of archaeological confirmation,[253] exactly fits the statement of William's biographer that in 1066 the Conqueror spent eight days at Dover adding to it those fortifications which it lacked (*Recepto castro, quae minus erant per dies octo addidit firmamenta*).[254] In short, the pre-Conquest *castel, castellum, castrum* at Dover was not a castle, and we meet here again one of the principal problems (much in need of attention)[255] for the historian of this period, namely the shifting sands of vocabulary. For feudal terminology at this date is still in the

---

[244] P. 24.
[245] For what follows, see Brown, *Arch. Journ.*, cxxvi. 144–5.
[246] Ed. Whitelock, 117–8; cf. Plummer, *Two of the Saxon Chronicles Parallel*, i. 175. Doc. 5.
[247] Thus e.g. Plummer, ii. 237; Stenton, *Anglo-Saxon England*, 555.
[248] Ed. Thorpe, i. 205–6. Doc. 15.
[249] Ed. Whitelock, 118; Plummer, i. 173.
[250] For Dover as an Iron Age fortress, see Armitage, 144; H. M. Colvin, *Antiquity*, xxxiii (1959).
[251] William of Poitiers, ed. Foreville, 104; Doc. 25. Harold promises to hand over to the duke *castrum Doveram*.
[252] William of Poitiers, ed. Foreville, 210–12 (Doc. 28); *Carmen de Hastingae Proelio*, ed. J. A. Giles, 44.
[253] *Arch. Journ.*, cxxvi. 145, citing the reports of Mr Martin Biddle.
[254] Ed. Foreville, 212. Doc. 28.
[255] Cf. p. 34 above.

process of development even in France, let alone in England where, in the nature of things, the process had scarcely begun. Usage is not yet regularized nor have words in all cases yet taken on their subsequent precise meanings, so that the *miles* of Domesday Book is not necessarily a knight, nor the *castel* of the Chronicle necessarily a castle.

If, inevitably, a large part of the argument for the absence of native castles in pre-Conquest England has to be based upon the negative or quasi-negative evidence emanating from that time and place, we can surely next add to it to complete the case the overwhelming and positive evidence of all kinds – literary, documentary, archaeological and even pictorial – for the huge programme of castle-building carried out by the Normans as from 1066. For why should this have been necessary if castles already existed? And if the Normans felt compelled to raise castles even in London (three) and York (two) or Winchester, the ancient chief city of Wessex, to say nothing of countless other places, it is clearly very difficult to sustain the argument for pre-Conquest English castles – and therefore feudalism. Castles raised across the length and breadth of the land, and by no means confined to frontier districts and strategic towns and cities, were in fact a principal means whereby the Norman Conquest was effected, rendered permanent, and the new Norman settlement rivetted upon the land, as the Norman King, his vassals and their vassals, almost literally dug or walled themselves in. Few things are more significantly striking in this respect than, say, an aerial photograph of Pleshey in Essex,[256] chosen by the new Norman Mandeville lords as the *caput* and head of their Essex honor, where everything is new – castle, subsidiary fortified township, even the new name Pleshey – the indelible imprint of the Norman Conquest and of the imposition of a new, alien and feudal ruling class upon the land. It is impossible to miss the contrast between the extreme paucity and exceptional nature of any references to castles before 1066, discussed above, and the endless references to them afterwards. Almost the first recorded act of the Normans on landing in 1066 was to raise a castle at Pevensey, to be followed by another at Hastings which the Bayeux Tapestry actually shows as being constructed.[257] The victory of October 14 was followed closely by the planting of a castle at Dover,[258] and subsequently others in London.[259] Thereafter the military and social progress of the Conquest and settlement is marked and measured by the castles which were raised – at Exeter in the far west, for example, in 1068 after the

---

[256] Doc. 79.
[257] William of Jumièges, 134 (Doc. 23); William of Poitiers, 168 (Doc. 26); *Anglo-Saxon Chronicle* 'D', ed. Whitelock, 143 (Doc. 9); *Bayeux Tapestry*, ed. Stenton, Pl. 51 (Doc.76).
[258] Above.
[259] William of Poitiers, 218, 236.

suppression of the rebellion of that city, or, later in the same year, at Warwick, Nottingham and York, Lincoln, Huntingdon and Cambridge, in the course of the Conqueror's first northern expedition and campaign.[260] Domesday Book adds its tale in the number of houses or tenements destroyed in some towns and cities to make way for the new castle – 166 at Lincoln, 113 at Norwich.[261] The complaints of the Anglo-Saxon Chronicle, now giving, as it were, the worm's eye view of the Conquest, are reiterated and bitter, reflecting one harsh aspect of reality in the association of castles with oppression. '[They] built castles far and wide throughout this country, and distressed the wretched folk, and always after that it grew much worse. May the end be good when God wills.'[262] In its obituary of King William himself it is stated simply

'He had castles built
And poor men hard oppressed,'[263]

while from another source we can still hear the curse of Archbishop Ealdred upon Urse d'Abbetot the sheriff for raising the new castle at Worcester so close to the church that its ditches encroached upon the monks' cemetery – 'Hattest thou Urs, have thou Godes kurs'.[264] By the end of the reign casual and unsystematic references in Domesday Book relate to some fifty castles in England and Wales and by the end of the century the number of castles in England alone to which we have reference in all the written sources so far searched amounts to eighty-four, though given the nature of those sources this will only be a portion of the whole.[265] An authentic glimpse of the network of castles which by then had sprung up as the focal points of military power, local government and lordship, is afforded by the Anglo-Saxon Chronicle in its account of the journey undertaken in the year 1074 by Edgar Æthling and his household from Scotland to William in Normandy – 'And the sheriff of York came to meet them at Durham and went all the way with them and had them provided with food and fodder at every castle they came to, until they got overseas to the King.'[266]

If all this is so – and it is – what then can be the reasons calling, in the words of a recent writer, for 'a complete rethinking of our ideas concerning the place of private fortification in the late Saxon state'?[267] The approach is primarily archaeological and the train of thought

[260] Brown, *Normans*, 235, with references given. Doc. 31.
[261] *Domesday Book*, i. 336b; ii. 116.
[262] Ed. Whitelock, 145. Doc. 11.
[263] Ibid., 164. Doc. 14.
[264] William of Malmesbury, *De Gestis Pontificum Anglorum*, ed. N.E.S.A. Hamilton (Rolls Series, London, 1870), 253. Doc. 33.
[265] Armitage, 94–5.
[266] Ed. Whitelock, 156. Doc. 12.
[267] Davison, *Arch. Journ.*, cxxiv. 207.

chiefly derives from the mere physical shape and form of certain early castles, thus taking insufficient note of those other considerations and other sorts of evidence necessary if the castle is to be seen in the round as the product and manifestation of a particular organization of society. Some early castles consisted of or incorporated stone buildings and defences from the beginning, but others, not least in the circumstances of the Norman Conquest of England, were simple, quicker, cheaper but scarcely less effective affairs of earthwork and timber. The best-known type of earthwork and timber castle is the so-called 'motte-and-bailey' castle, where to the ditched, banked and palisaded enclosure of the bailey there is added the self-contained and dominant feature of the motte, a great mound of earth (artificial, natural or both), with its own ditch and bank at the base, and a palisade, probably enclosing a timber tower, about the summit.[268] But the attention of archaeologists is currently being directed to another type of earthwork and timber castle which had no motte, a straightforward enclosure of ditch, bank and palisade, and which, as indeed Mrs Armitage pointed out long ago, may have been the original type in Normandy.[269] To these the totally unsatisfactory and misleading name of 'ringworks' is in process of being given,[270] and from them much confusion threatens to arise. For if some of the earliest Norman castles were mere enclosures of this kind, and if the residences of pre-Conquest English thegns were also enclosed in some way, as they presumably were, then wherein lies the difference?

The question thus posed is easy enough to answer. The difference lies in the intention and hence the scale, strength and design of the enclosure. The dividing line between the castle, that is the fortified residence, and the unfortified residence is always going to be hazy, but on either side of that dividing line there is really no confusion. There is a substantial difference between, let us say, your garden fence – or even wall – and mine, on the one hand, and the walls of Caernarvon Castle on the other. Again, my own part of the world in north Suffolk is full of medieval moated sites, moated homesteads, but no one, contemporary or historian, has ever called them castles: their moats served to enclose and demarcate a property, to keep animals in and out, to discourage criminal rather than hostile military intrusion. The truth is that medieval bureaucrats and civil servants no less than modern historians had difficulty in knowing where to draw the line between fortification and mere enclosure, between

---

[268] Docs. 76, 79.

[269] Armitage, 78, *n.* 1, and cf. p. 70. Cf. Doc. 78.

[270] For current reviews of the subject see D. J. C. King and L. Alcock, 'Ringworks of England and Wales,' and B. K. Davison, 'Early earthwork castles: a new model,' both in *Château-Gaillard* III, the latter using the more satisfactory term 'enclosure castles'.

the castle and the unfortified residence. In England in the later Middle Ages crenellation (battlements) was evidently taken as the criterion, and you needed a licence for it (hence licences to crenellate). In Normandy and Anglo-Norman England in the second half of the eleventh century the evidence suggests that the criteria included the depth of ditches and the height of banks, the strength and design of palisades. A document of 1091, known as the Customs and Rights (*Consuetudines et Justicie*) of the duke of Normandy and setting down the rights and powers of the duke in the time of William the Conqueror, has an interesting clause dealing with the ducal control of fortification within the duchy. No one, we are roundly told, may make a castle (*castellum facere*) in Normandy (presumably, without ducal licence), and no one in the open country is to dig a fosse or ditch of more than one shovel's throw in depth, nor make a palisade of more than one line or with battlements and wall-walks.[271]

One difficulty relative to the revived question of the presence or absence of castles in pre-Conquest England is that (no doubt significantly enough) it has so far proved difficult to identify the sites of Old English thegnly residences in order that they may be archaeologically investigated – though some royal sites are known and, as noted above, are not fortified.[272] At Sulgrave in Northamptonshire, however, there is reason to believe that an early post-Conquest 'ringwork' occupies the site of such a pre-Conquest thegnly residence – and hence its near-unique interest. The excavations[273] there are still proceeding at the time of writing and therefore the matter is *sub judice*, but the most significant point to emerge as yet is that 'the plan of the late Saxon enclosure differed radically from that of the later [*i.e.* post-Conquest] ringwork' though beyond that its form is unknown.[274] If, therefore (and in the absence of documentary evidence that fact also is unknown) Sulgrave rated as a castle after 1066, it looks very much as though it achieved that status by virtue of bigger and better banks and ditches, and, no doubt, palisades.

One piece of literary or documentary evidence has also been adduced in favour of the possibility of private fortifications, i.e. castles, in pre-Conquest England. This is the compilation known as 'Of People's Ranks and Laws' (which in fact we have met before),[275] a kind of moral tract for the times, probably compiled by Archbishop Wulfstan of York

[271] Cap. 4. Printed in C. H. Haskins, *Norman Institutions* (New York, 1918), 282. Doc. 62.
[272] Above, p. 73.
[273] Under the direction of B. K. Davison. For interim reports and comment, see *Château-Gaillard*, II, 45–6; *Arch. Journ.*, cxxiv. 208–9; *Medieval Archaeology*, v. 328; vi–vii. 333; viii. 237; xiii. 236; *Current Archaeology*, ii. 19–22.
[274] *Arch. Journ.*, cxxvi. 143–4.
[275] Above, p. 45.

between 1002 and 1023.[276] The passage in question relates to the qualifications of thegnhood, which could be achieved by the peasant who
sufficiently prospered, and reads as follows: 'If a ceorl prospered, so that
he possessed fully five hides of land of his own (church and kitchen),[277]
a bell and a *burh-geat*,[278] a seat and special office in the king's hall, then
was he thenceforth of thegn-right worthy.' It has been suggested (perhaps optimistically) that this definition of a thegn is expressed 'in terms
which would seem almost designed to facilitate archaeological iden-
tification', and further, and more important, that the reference here to
the *burh-geat* implies that the thegnly residence was defensive, fortified –
'the crucial word here is *burhgeat* . . . a thegn was expected to boast
some form of private defended [*sic*] enclosure or *burh*, in which stood
his chapel and other buildings. That the entrance to this enclosure
should be singled out for mention rather than the enclosure itself
implies that this gate was of some elaboration.' The crucial question has
then been posed, albeit in loaded terms – 'The question is, of course,
to what extent can a private defended [*sic*] residence of this sort be
called a castle?'[279]

But the point is that there is no evidence here for the defence or
fortification of the thegnly residence. A gateway, be it never so grand,
does not make a castle, then or now. In any case, for the text cited to
refer to the *burh* only in terms of the *burh-geat* may seem a curious way
to refer it at all, and for the gate thus to be singled out alone for a
mention, and in association with a bell, may imply less that it was archi-
tecturally of some elaboration and more that it fulfilled some lordly and
symbolic function – perhaps, as Maitland thought, the dispensation of
justice.[280] Further, we are clearly here caught in the treacherous sands
of terminology again and must investigate the meaning of *burh*, in
modern English 'burgh' or 'borough'. If we do, we find that while a

[276] Stubbs, *Select Charters*, 88; *English Historical Documents*, i. 432; F.
Liebermann, *Die Gesetze der Angelsachsen* (Halle, 1903–16), i. 456. Doc. 60.

[277] The words in parenthesis are omitted from some texts.

[278] Translated without comment in *English Historical Documents* as 'castle-
gate'. Cf. p. 34 above.

[279] Davison, *Arch. Journ.*, cxxiv. 204. At Sulgrave a stone building of the pre-
Conquest period, measuring some 33 feet by 30 feet and standing to a height of
7 feet, buried in the post-Conquest rampart, seemed at one time a possible
example of the enigmatic *burh-geat*. It seems likely, however, that this pre-
Conquest tower (presumably with a timber superstructure) was converted into
a somewhat unsatisfactory gate-tower at the time of the post-Conquest remodel-
ling of the site. In any case its very slender walls, only some 22 inches thick,
scarcely support any theory that Sulgrave was a fortified residence before 1066.
See *Medieval Archaeology*, xiii. 236; *Current Archaeology*, ii. No. 1, January
1969.

[280] *Domesday Book and Beyond*, 232, n. 3. Cf. the early twelfth-century legal
treatise, the *Leges Henrici Primi*, cap. 16 – 'Thus far shall the king's peace extend
from his *burhgeat* where he is sitting . . .', Maitland, 226.

root meaning of the word is certainly 'fortification, fortified place',[281] the noun itself is derived from the Old Teutonic verb *bergan*, to shelter or protect,[282] and thus while the word *burh* was used from an early date to signify a military encampment, a fortified place, so also it was used to signify the enclosure about a residence,[283] without any implication of military fortification at all. The latter usage is abundantly illustrated in Old English laws, not least in relation to *burgbryce*, the offence of breaking into such enclosures, i.e. forcible entry, for which a compensatory payment or *bot* was payable to the injured party (hence *burgbot*). In this way Ine's laws in the late seventh century refer to the *burh* or *burg* of the king, the bishop, the ealdorman and the nobleman,[284] and this at a date (688–94) long before castles had been invented on the Continent, let alone in England. Similar instances could be multiplied from the laws of other pre-Conquest kings,[285] while it should be noted from the same code of Ine that a ceorl's premises, that is his homestead (the word used is *worthig*), are also to be enclosed, the reason mentioned being to prevent the straying of beasts – 'A ceorl's premises shall be fenced both winter and summer. If they are not enclosed, and a beast belonging to his neighbour strays in through the opening he has left, he shall have no claim on that beast, [but] he shall drive it out and suffer the damage.'[286] The *burh* of the legal texts is evidently the English equivalent of the continental *manse* or *mansus* of Carolingian capitularies, described by its latest historian as 'an enclosure, solidly rooted to its site by a permanent barrier such as a palisade or a living hedge, carefully maintained, a protected asylum to which the entry was forbidden and the violation of which was punished by severe penalties. . . .'[287] Though in the Old English laws the word *burh* in this sense appears to be confined to the upper classes, the peasant had his equivalent in his homestead: both were enclosed, both were protected at law, but neither was fortified, and the offence against them which the legislators had in mind was what we should call housebreaking or trespass, not a military assault by armed forces.

[281] A. H. Smith, *English Place-Name Elements*, Pt. I (English Place-Name Society, xxv, 1956), 58ff.
[282] *New English Dictionary*. Cf. Armitage, 17.
[283] Cf. Maitland, *Domesday Book and Beyond*, 225, 227.
[284] Cap. 45: Stubbs, *Select Charters*, 68; *English Historical Documents*, i. 369; F. L. Attenborough, *Laws of the Earliest English Kings* (New York, 1963), 50, 51; Doc. 55. It will be noticed that Attenborough's rendering of *burg* as 'fortified premises' has no real justification.
[285] E.g. Alfred, cap. 40: *English Historical Documents*, i. 379; Attenborough, 82, 83; Doc. 57. Cf. *Arch. Journ.*, cxxvi. 142. Alfred, like Ine (below), uses a different, less elevated word for the ceorl's enclosure, viz *edor*, i.e. 'fence'.
[286] Cap. 40. *English Historical Documents*, i. 368; Attenborough, 48, 49. Doc. 54.
[287] Georges Duby, *Rural Economy and Country Life in the Medieval West* (translated C. Postan, London, 1968), 7.

Anglo-Norman Feudalism a Norman Innovation

THERE is thus no acceptable evidence for native castles in pre-Conquest England, nor, as we have seen, is there for indigenous knights, nor for vassalic commendation, nor the fee. Without any of these four fundamentals of feudal society, the argument for pre-Conquest English feudalism not only cannot be sustained, it cannot be begun. Whence, then, came English feudalism? No one has ever sought to deny the feudal structure of English society and the kingdom a century after the Norman Conquest, in the second half of the twelfth century, in the light of the comparatively abundant evidence then available; nor, for that matter, in the reign of Stephen; nor under Henry I, whose reign begins with a coronation charter full of the 'feudal incidents' of relief, wardship and marriage – promising remedies for their abuse as it promises also quittance of geld upon the demesne of knights holding their lands 'by the hauberk' (holding *fiefs de haubert*);[1] nor even under Rufus, whose notorious writ of 1095, for example, is unequivocal evidence for the imposition by then of feudal tenure, with all its burdens, upon the church – 'Know that, the bishop being dead, the honor [*i.e.* the bishopric] has come back into my hand.'[2] Here surely, even in these few instances, we meet at once the new terminology of new institutions; but the gradualists in the matter of their origin have necessarily always relied heavily upon pre-Conquest precedents to explain their slow, development. Without those – and they do not exist – then, as Stubbs albeit a gradualist himself, was constrained to remark, 'there is a difference which the short interval of time will not account for'.[3] And

---

[1] Cc. 2, 3, 4, 11. Printed in Stubbs, *Select Charters*, 118–9; *English Historical Documents*, ii. ed. D. C. Douglas (London, 1959), 401–2. Doc. 52. For the so-called 'feudal incidents' of relief, wardship and marriage, see below p. 91.

[2] Stubbs, *Select Charters*, 109; full text in Round, *Feudal England*, 309. Doc. 51.

[3] William Stubbs, *Constitutional History of England* (5th. ed., 1891), i. 283. For Stubbs it was '[not] easy to reduce the organization described in Domesday to strict conformity with feudal law as it appears later', and in consequence his interval was limited to that between Domesday in 1086 and the accession of Henry I in 1100, which is short indeed.

setting aside, as well we may, the improbable attempt of Freeman, based upon the more cautious suggestions of Stubbs,[4] to attribute English feudalism to the ingenious and diabolical invention of Ranulf Flambard and William Rufus,[5] where else are we to look for its origins if not to the suitably cataclysmic occasion of the Norman Conquest? Feudalism we have seen to be an upper-class affair, associated in particular with an upper-class tenure of land in return for military service, knight-service: the direct and almost immediate result of the Conquest was the near-total replacement of the Old English land-lord and land-owning class by a new one from northern France and more especially Normandy.[6]

That Norman society itself was feudal in the mid-eleventh century cannot really be denied, though the implication is sometimes found in attempts to undermine the thesis that English feudalism is a Norman importation. The approach tends to be the seemingly scholarly one that the evidence from pre-Conquest Normandy is not enough to show the existence then of a fully developed and uniform system of tenure by knight-service, with all quotas assessed and obligations defined.[7] Yet the reality of Norman feudalism in 1066 is not to be doubted because it had not then achieved the further stage of development largely induced by the special circumstances of the Conquest itself. The evidence is more than sufficient to show the presence and prominence of all four fundamentals of feudalism in pre-Conquest Normandy – knight, fief, castle and vassalic commendation – and Haskins' conclusion that 'Norman society in 1066 was a feudal society, and one of the most fully

---

[4] The full passage in Stubbs (as above) reads as follows – 'Between the picture drawn in Domesday and the state of affairs which the charter of Henry I was designed to remedy, there is a difference which the short interval of time will not account for, and which testifies to the action of some skilful organising hand working with neither justice nor mercy, hardening and sharpening all lines and points to the perfecting of strong government'. For Flambard, see ibid., 324–8.

[5] Both in his *Norman Conquest* (1867–79) and his *Reign of William Rufus* (Oxford, 1882). The whole matter, with appropriate references and quotations, is succinctly dealt with by Round (*Feudal England*, 225–31), who justly observed in passing that Freeman 'had an equal horror of Ranulf Flambard and of the "feudal system"'.

[6] By 1087 there were only two prominent English landholders left, and only three native prelates in the English church (Stenton, *Anglo-Saxon England*, 618, 671; Loyn, *Norman Conquest*, 171–2; Brown, *Normans*, 204ff.)

[7] A balanced discussion of the point will be found in D. C. Douglas, *William the Conqueror* (London, 1964), 96–104. This includes (p. 97) a carefully worded conclusion that, 'There thus seems little warranty for believing that anything resembling tenure by knight-service, in the later sense of the term, was uniformly established, or carefully defined, in pre-Conquest Normandy', which if carefully interpreted does nothing to undermine the established view of the Norman origin of English feudalism. Cf. therefore the review of Douglas by D. J. A. Matthew, *English Historical Review*, lxxxvi. 562.

developed feudal societies in Europe', has recently been restated by one of its latest historians in almost the same words.[8] There is also the powerful analogy of the introduction of feudalism in this same period by the Normans into southern Italy and subsequently Antioch, categorized together with England by Marc Bloch as countries of imported feudalism – with the highly relevant remark that 'In the countries where feudalism was an importation it was much more systematically organized than in those where its development had been purely spontaneous'.[9] Our problem, therefore, reduced to its simplest terms, appears to resolve itself into an equation with an answer which there seems no reason to avoid – non-feudal pre-Conquest England, plus feudal pre-Conquest Normandy, equals feudal post-Conquest Anglo-Norman England.

Round, arguing his cataclysmic thesis of the introduction of knight-service, and therefore feudalism, as the sudden result of the Norman Conquest, against the gradualists of his own day, observed that 'the assumption that the Conqueror cannot have introduced any new principle in the tenure of land lies at the root of the matter'.[10] It evidently does, for one of his most recent critics returns to the attack armed with the same assumption – 'it is altogether incredible that the Conqueror introduced an entirely novel military obligation'.[11] Yet what more likely an occasion for a tenurial and, with it, military revolution than the circumstance and *tabula rasa* of the Norman Conquest? The Norman settlement of England comprised a social revolution in the upper levels of society and the partitioning of the land, under the close direction of the Norman duke and king, among a French and Norman aristocracy, both parties likely to continue here the customs and habits of their homeland, and both alike constrained above all to respond to immediate necessity. In the early days at least the Norman Conquest was the military occupation of a potentially hostile country still threatened by Scandinavian claimants,[12] and the imposition of a small, alien ruling class of perhaps ten thousand upon a native population of about one and a half million.[13] It should be realized, perhaps more often than it is, that

[8] Haskins, *Norman Institutions*, 5. Cf. Michel de Boüard, *Guillaume le Conquérant* (Paris, 1958), 61. For a survey of the evidence of pre-Conquest Norman feudalism, see Brown, *Normans*, 39–49. In addition to Haskins, two pieces of fundamental work upon early Norman feudalism are by H. Navel: 'L'enquête de 1133 sur les fiefs de l'evêché de Bayeux' and 'Recherches sur les institutions féodales en Normandie (Région de Caen)', respectively in *Bulletin de la Société des Antiquaires de Normandie*, xlii (1934) and li (1952).

[9] Bloch, 187–8. For the Normans in Italy see C. Cahen, *Le régime féodal en Italie normande* (Paris, 1940).

[10] *Feudal England*, 247.

[11] D. J. A. Matthew, *The Norman Conquest* (London, 1966), 117.

[12] Until at least 1085–6. See Stenton, *Anglo-Saxon England*, 608–9.

[13] Brown, *Normans*, 211 and n. 36.

while the arrangements then made to cope with the situation were to mould society into a feudal pattern to last for centuries, they were less the conscious introduction of 'the feudal system', and more the spontaneous reaction to immediate and urgent needs.

Refuge is often taken by those seeking to deny any dramatic change following the Conquest in the comparative paucity of evidence for the Conqueror's reign, and more especially in an alleged silence of the chronicles on the imposition of a new and expensive burden of military service upon the land and not least upon the Church. Thus Freeman wrote, 'There is no ground then for thinking that William directly or systematically introduced any new kind of tenure into the holding of English lands. There is nothing to suggest any such belief, either in the Chronicles of his reign, in the Survey which is his greatest monument, in the genuine, or even in the spurious, remains of his legislation.'[14] The passage is quoted with approval, for example, by Eric John, who goes on particularly to stress 'This silence in an age full of excellent chroniclers', and to adduce 'the silence of Ordericus Vitalis' amongst others, as 'an argument of weight'.[15] In fact, the evidence for the condition of King William's England, like the evidence for the England of King Edward's day, may not be abundant, but it is again more than sufficient to show the overall pattern,[16] and the contrast between the two becomes the more obvious the more closely it is studied. The overwhelming evidence for the planting of castles in and after 1066 as part and parcel of the Norman Conquest and settlement has already been rehearsed.[17] So too has Round's argument, and evidence, including the Evesham writ, for the imposition of the quotas by the Conqueror, and the introduction of knight-service distinct from and extra to the Old English fyrd service which in any case was continued after 1066,[18] while there is much evidence to show that the secondary and subsequent process of subinfeudation by the tenants-in-chief themselves had gone far by the time of Domesday Book in 1086.[19] As for the Survey itself, it may indeed be (together, let us say, with the Tower of London or St Albans Cathedral) the Conqueror's 'greatest monument', but it was misinterpreted by Freeman as by Stubbs. It stands in fact, in the words of

[14] Norman Conquest, v (1876), 372.
[15] Land Tenure in Early England, 152–3. So, too, Matthew, Norman Conquest, n. 54 to 117. For what follows, cf. Round, Feudal England, 298–308; Hollister, Military Organization of Norman England, 25–8; J. O. Prestwich, Past and Present, No. 26, 44; Brown, Normans, 223ff.
[16] Cf. p. 33 above.
[17] Above, pp. 72 ff.
[18] Above, pp. 62 ff. For the writ, see Doc. 47.
[19] Below. Cf. Brown, Normans, 218; Stenton, First Century, 136; Hollister, Military Organization of Norman England, 54–5; Hollings, English Historical Review, lxiii. 463; Douglas, Feudal Documents from the Abbey of Bury St. Edmunds (London, 1932), lxxxv.

one of its latest historians, as 'the formal written record of the introduction of feudal tenure, and therefore of feudal law into England',[20] for quite apart from its casual references to fees and honors, knights and castles, the huge corpus of information it contains, largely obtained from the ancient administrative units of vills and hundreds, was laboriously re-arranged in terms of tenure, royal demesne and tenants-in-chief county by county, and writ large upon every page is the pure feudal doctrine of *nulle terre sans seigneur*, and the feudal principle that all land is held of the king, now also the feudal suzerain. (Doc. 71.)

Nor are the chroniclers silent on these matters, nor lacking in complaints at the imposition of new knight-services upon the Church. It may well be that the incidence of the latter in practice can be exaggerated, for the lands of the church, like all the land of England, had long been charged with the military service of the fyrd, and in so far as the real importance of the fyrd declined after 1066 by so much would the new knight-service be less an extra burden.[21] In some cases at least in the first generation also, knight-service must have seemed more the personal obligation of the new tenants of Church lands – of whom we hear a good deal[22] – than an imposition on the churches themselves, while, of course, the cumulative appointments of Norman clerics to bishoprics, abbeys and other ecclesiastical dignities would do much to temper criticism or resentment. It so happens, too, that the reign of William the Conqueror (as well as that of Rufus) far from being 'an age full of excellent chroniclers', is one peculiarly devoid of good contemporary narrative sources. On the one hand, the Anglo-Saxon Chronicle, ever an over-rated authority, declines further after 1066 to the point of becoming chiefly valuable as a kind of worm's-eye view of the Conquest, while, on the other, of the principal contemporary Norman chroniclers, William of Jumièges ends in 1072 and the text of William of Poitiers as we have it breaks off in 1067. The great age of Anglo-Norman chroniclers (itself not the least valuable of the results of the Norman Conquest) does not begin until the earlier twelfth century. Nevertheless we hear rather more than silence. In its own terms, the native Chronicle refers to an early aspect of the Norman land settlement in its reference to the submission of the English leaders who 'afterwards bought their lands'.[23] while William of Poitiers in the one year for which his text survives after Hastings speaks both of the rich fiefs (*opulenta beneficia*)

[20] V. H. Galbraith, *The Making of Domesday Book* (Oxford, 1961), 160 and cf· 28–30.

[21] Brown, *Normans*, 223; Prestwich, *Past and Present*, No. 26, p. 47.

[22] Cf. e.g. Round, *Feudal England*, 301–3; Miller, *Abbey and Bishopric of Ely*, 66ff. Thus at Ely the abbot enfeoffed the 'intruders' upon the abbey lands 'so that they would serve the king in all military expeditions and the Church be henceforth untroubled' (*Liber Eliensis*, ed. E. O. Blake, 217, and Doc. 37).

[23] Ed. Whitelock, 142, 'E'. Doc. 10.

which the new King granted to the castellans of his new castles, and specifically of the vassalic commendation rendered by archbishop Stigand to the victor of Hastings (*manibus ei sese dedit, fidem sacramento confirmavit* – i.e. homage and fealty).[24] If, *faute de mieux*, we turn to the writers of the next generation, we find the alleged silence of the incomparable Ordericus Vitalis shattered by the specific statement that William the Conqueror 'allocated lands to knights in such a way and so arranged their contingents that the kingdom of England should always have 60,000 knights at the ready and produce them immediately at the King's command as necessity required'.[25] We do not have to take literally the figure of 60,000 which is some ten times the reality[26] and simply stands for a great number, but otherwise the statement, made after a detailed description of the distribution of lands by William to his companions in *c.*1071 after the fall of Ely,[27] is explicit enough, and the implied date convincing.[28]

Two later and local monastic chroniclers of twelfth-century England also, each not obviously unreliable, each, to put it mildly, closer to these events than we are, and each steeped in the tradition and recent history of his house, explicitly refer to the imposition of knight-service upon the English Church in general and its effect upon their own churches in particular. The Abingdon Chronicle, states categorically concerning the Norman Conquest that, 'after the disturbances had died down . . . it was noted in the annals [*in Annalibus annotaretur*] by the king's command how many knights should be exacted from bishops and abbots for the defence of the realm when need should arise', and goes on to describe the necessary subinfeudations which abbot Athelhelm subsequently made, from land formerly held of the Church by thegns who had fallen at Hastings, in each case 'in return for stipulated service from the manor thus given'.[29] The same chronicler also leaves no doubt that the feudal knight-service of castle-guard, which the abbey is known from later evidence to have owed at Windsor, was imposed upon it by William the Conqueror soon after 1066.[30] Similarly the *Liber Eliensis* or the Book of Ely states that the king for his Scottish campaign in 1072 demanded the knight-service due from the bishops and abbots of England, which

[24] Ed. Foreville, 216, 238. Docs. 29, 30.

[25] Ed. Chibnall, ii. 267. Doc. 32.

[26] Cf. Round (290–2) whose own figure for the total number of knights obtained from the quotas was *c.* 5000. A. L. Poole estimated 6–7000 (*Obligations of Society in the Twelfth and Thirteenth Centuries*, Oxford, 1946, 36).

[27] Ordericus Vitalis, ed. Chibnall, ii. 261–7.

[28] Cf. the Evesham, Ely and St Albans evidence below.

[29] *Chronicon Monasterii de Abingdon*, ed. J. Stevenson (Rolls Series, London, 1858), ii. 3; *English Historical Documents*, ii. 902; Doc. 36. Duly cited by Round, 299–300. The curious 'in Annalibus annotaretur' may perhaps be compared with the *inrotulans* of Matthew Paris, cited below.

[30] Ibid., Doc. 36.

service was henceforward to be the perpetual right of the Crown,[31] and later states that in the first year of his reign William Rufus demanded from the churches the due service (*debitum servitium* – the very textbook phrase) which his father had imposed upon them.[32] The Ely chronicler, moreover, makes it very clear that the complaints of the abbey were loud and long at the new imposition, but to no avail, a personal visit by Abbot Simeon to the king himself resulting only in the royal command to garrison the Isle with forty knights (i.e. the later known *servitium debitum* of the church of Ely).[33] Finally, in this not inconsiderable corpus of explicit chronicle evidence, there is the testimony of Matthew Paris – following Roger of Wendover and both writing in the thirteenth century – that in the year 1070 the Conqueror imposed military service upon the bishoprics and abbeys holding baronies, enrolling (*inrotulans*) the number of knights due from each according to his will.[34] It is not true, as Matthew states, that the Church had hitherto been free of secular service (though in his day 'secular service' might do as a loose synonym for knight-service which the Church had certainly not known before), and much scorn has been poured on Round's use of this late sources to prove events two hundred years before.[35] Yet as Round showed, and we have shown, the statement of Matthew Paris, coming from the historian of the well-informed house of St Albans, does not stand alone; it is consistent with the other evidence both as to substance and as to date; and Matthew, again and like his predecessors at Abingdon and Ely, stood somewhat closer to the Conquest and its still living tradition than comfortable modern disbelievers in cataclysmic change.

There is also written evidence for the introduction of feudalism in the Conqueror's reign of a different sort from, and in a sense even more direct than, the statements and allusions of chroniclers or the overall implication of Domesday Book. Charters of enfeoffment are of course rare in the early post-Conquest period, not because enfeoffments were rare, but because secular society in particular still placed its trust in visual and physical ceremony before witnesses – commendation with investiture and seisin – rather than in written documents for the conveyance of property. Nevertheless, before they become increasingly

---

[31] *Liber Eliensis*, ed. E. O. Blake (Camden 3rd. Series, xcii, London, 1962), 216. Doc. 37. Cf. Round, 299.

[32] Ibid., 218; Doc. 37. Cf. Round, 299.

[33] Ibid., 217; Doc. 37. Round, 299, n. 231.

[34] Matthew Paris, *Historia Anglorum*, ed. F. Madden (Rolls Series, London, 1866–9), i. 13: cf. Wendover, *Flores Historiarum*, ed. H.O. Coxe, (London 1841–4), ii. 7. Doc.38. Cited by Round (p. 298), who led off his section of chronicle evidence with it.

[35] Thus Eric John, *Land Tenure*, 153; Richardson and Sayles, *Governance of Medieval England*, 62ff. Matthew, *Norman Conquest*, n. 54, p. 117.

common in the course of the twelfth century, a few survive even from
the first generation of the Conquest, and they speak in a language not
heard before 1066 of a new feudal tenure and new feudal institutions.
One such, a well-known charter from the abbey of Bury St Edmunds in
Suffolk, opens with the statement that 'Peter, a knight (*miles*) of king
William, will be the feudal man (*feodalis homo*) of St. Edmund and
abbot Baldwin by homage (*manibus junctis*)', and goes on to speak of the
fief (*feodum*) which Peter will hold of the Abbot in return for the knight-
service which he will render to him (*cum tribus vel quattuor militibus*).[36]
Another, by Robert Losinga, Bishop of Hereford, and dated 1085,
records the enfeoffment of Roger de Lacy, knight (*miles*), by the counsel
of the Bishop's men (*consilio suorum*, i.e. the Bishop's honorial court),
with land from the Bishop's demesne (*proprio dominio*) at Holme (subsequently Holme Lacy) for the service of two knights (*ut duobus militibus
serviet sibi*), as Roger's father had held it before him.[37] A third, by Gilbert Crispin, Abbot of Westminster, records the grant to William
Baynard of land at Westminster, 'to hold for the whole of his life for the
service of one knight (*pro servicio unius militis*)'; William is to have in the
land all the customs and liberties of the church of Westminster except
tithes and except the 'aids' which the Church receives from its knights
(*exceptis auxiliis nostris que inde . . . de militibus nostris accipiemus*).[38]
Other charters and documents surviving from the Conqueror's reign,
though not relating to enfeoffment, similarly and increasingly employ the
language of feudalism, as when Robert Malet, in his foundation charter
for his priory of Eye in Suffolk, both refers to his castle (*castellum*) at Eye
and grants to his monks 'all the other liberties which my lord William
king of England granted to me when he gave me the honor (*quando
honorem mihi dedit*)',[39] or as when in the King's writs the barons and
knights of the shire take the place of the thegns of old.[40]

That two out of the three surviving charters of enfeoffment cited –
that of Robert Losinga to Roger de Lacy, and that of Gilbert Crispin

[36] Printed in Douglas, *Feudal Documents from the Abbey of Bury St. Edmunds*,
151, No. 168; *English Historical Documents*, ii. 896. Doc. 48. The explanation of
the King's interest in instances of subinfeudation is perhaps more likely to be
that suggested by Miller (*Abbey and Bishopric of Ely*, 67 and n. 2) than by
Douglas (*Feudal Documents*, xcvff.).
[37] Printed with facsimile and commentary by V. H. Galbraith, 'An Episcopal
Land-Grant of 1085,' *English Historical Review*, xliv. 1929; *English Historical
Documents*, ii. 897. Doc. 50.
[38] Printed by J. Armitage Robinson, *Gilbert Crispin, abbot of Westminster*, 38;
English Historical Documents, ii. 895. Doc. 49. For 'aid' see p. 91 below.
[39] Cartulary of Eye Priory, Essex Record Office, f. 17v. Stenton, *First Century*,
56, n. 3. Robert Malet probably succeeded his father, William, soon after 1071.
[40] H. W. C. Davis, *Regesta Regum Anglo-Normannorum*, i (Oxford, 1913), e.g.
Nos. 43, 122, 175, 185, 202, 215, 221; Appendix, Nos. III, IX, XXIII, XXV,
XXX.

to William Baynard – explicitly convey a life tenancy only should occasion no surprise, for in the beginning the fief was not hereditary, nor was it to become so in English law before the reign of Henry II whatever may have been the practice increasingly dictated by social pressure.[41] Hence in large part the huge power of feudal 'patronage', the ability to make and break, to cast down as well as to set up, greatest of all in the hands of the King who is the greatest feudal lord of all, and stemming ultimately from the fact that as from 1066 all the magnates of the realm are his conditional tenants.[42] Hence, too, the relief of Rufus' writ and Henry I's coronation charter,[43] for the heir or incoming tenant must pay to have seisin and investiture of the fief. The fief reverts to the lord on the death of the vassal, and the rights of feudal lordship also include at least the custody of the fief during minority, together with the custody or wardship of minors, the control of their marriages and the control of the marriages of heiresses and widows. The so-called feudal 'incidents' of relief, wardship and marriage[44] loom large in Henry I's charter of liberties as they do in Magna Carta a century later, and a principal theme of English constitutional and political history as from 1066 is the continuing process of the definition, and thereby limitation of the feudal rights of lords, especially kings. These rights were valuable in terms of hard cash as well as of political and social patronage. Relief was a directly monetary payment, the escheat and custody of fiefs brought the revenues as well as the possession thereof, and wardships and marriages could be and were either granted for a sum or sold on the open market. Feudalism in these respects was still big business with the Court of Wards of Tudor and early Stuart monarchs, and if we add that knight-service itself could be, at the King's discretion, commuted for a money payment from an early date (scutage, shield-money, first heard of in 1100),[45] and that a tenant by knight-service owed to his lord financial 'aid', *auxilium* (referred to in Gilbert Crispin's charter), i.e.

[41] Ganshof, *Feudalism*, 43ff., 119ff. Cf. R. H. C. Davis, 'What Happened in Stephen's Reign?', *History*, xlix (1964). The final acceptance of the hereditary principle in the descent of fiefs in English law is marked by Henry II's assize of Morte d'Ancestor which protects the rights of heirs to succeed.

[42] An oft quoted passage from Ordericus Vitalis is apposite here, of how Henry I put down the mighty from their seats and set up others favourable to him in their place, albeit of ignoble birth, raised 'as I shall say, from the dust' (*Historia Ecclesiastica*, ed. A. le Prévost, iv. 164; Stubbs, *Select Charters*, 113). For the huge power of patronage wielded by Henry I (under whom, however, such powers neither began nor ended), see R. W. Southern, 'The Place of Henry I in English History,' *Proceedings of the British Academy*, xlviii (1963).

[43] Above, p. 83 and Docs. 51, 52.

[44] For which see A. L. Poole, *Obligations of Society in the Twelfth and Thirteenth Centuries*, 94ff.; Pollock and Maitland, *History of English Law*, i. 288ff.

[45] Poole, *Obligations of Society*, 40–1; Stenton, *First Century*, 177.

the service of his purse as well as that of his body,[46] we begin to see to what extent the advent of feudalism added to the resources and the powers of lords, the King especially – for throughout the Middle Ages, as from 1066, the King was beyond compare the greatest feudal lord of all. There never was so pernicious a heresy, so difficult to eradicate, as the insane concept that feudalism is a 'bad thing' to be suppressed as incompatible with monarchy.

Though the more one moves forward from 1066, the more the year appears in perspective as a watershed in English history, we must revert to the matter of the direct evidence for the introduction of English feudalism at the Conquest with the remark that there is more to knights than their enfeoffment and the obligations upon them of tenure by knight-service. The knight, the very essence of feudalism, is anterior to the fee, which is merely one method of his maintenance.[47] At any time in feudal England there will be more knights than fees, as younger sons and young men on the make abound, and stipendiary knights, taking service with a lord and serving for maintenance and pay, in the hope or expectation of a fief (or an heiress), are a common and permanent feature of feudal society in all periods. (They are the 'bachelors', young men not yet established, and therefore not yet married). Certainly it was so in Norman England in the beginning, though the household knight is not, for the reasons just given (yet as is so often stated or implied), a peculiar feature of the early years of the Conquest. The ethos of this new society, as well as the unsettled conditions of the times, required that a lord should have a retinue of knights, and thus the sources show them to us in the households of their lords as well as in the Conqueror's armies or enfeoffed upon the land. Ordericus Vitalis, in a memorable description of Hugh d'Avranches, Earl of Chester from at least 1077, remarks that he always moved about with an army rather than a household.[48] William of Malmesbury refers to the 'multitude of knights' maintained by William fitz Osbern, Earl of Hereford and the Conqueror's friend, who rewarded them so liberally as to irritate the King.[49] The Abingdon Chronicle states how Abbot Athelhelm 'in the early days of his coming to the abbey went nowhere unless surrounded by a force of armed knights', though when times became more settled he enfeoffed his knights upon lands belonging to the church,[50] while at Ely a similar

[46] For aids, see Pollock and Maitland, *History of English Law*, i. 330–2.

[47] Above, p. 24.

[48] Ed. Chibnall, ii. 260 – *non familiam secum sed exercitum semper ducebat*. Though strictly irrelevant to our purpose, one cannot resist quoting Ordericus' next memorable remark about this memorable Norman earl, that 'his hunting was a daily devastation of his lands' (ibid., 262, 263). See Doc. 32.

[49] *Gesta Regum*, ed. Stubbs (Rolls Series), ii. 314.

[50] *Chronicon Monasterii de Abingdon*, ii. 3; *English Historical Documents*, ii. 902; Doc. 36.

sequence of events took place, the Abbot at first 'maintained according to custom the number of knights predetermined by the king's command' (*habuit ex consuetudine secundum iussum regis pretaxatum militie numerum* – the wording seems instructive as relevant to the imposition of the quotas) in the claustral buildings until this proved prejudicial to good order and monastic discipline.[51] In these last two sources we thus obtain a precious glimpse of subinfeudation, and the same process was, of course, followed by secular lords in accordance with social pressure and the need to reward their own followers. Yet the stipendiary knight and the military household remained a feature of Norman and Anglo-Norman society and the custom was even adopted by surviving English lords. So Wulfstan, Bishop of Worcester, that paragon of Old English virtues, according to William of Malmesbury copied the Normans in this respect, and led in his train a retinue of knights (*pompam militum secum ducens*)[52] – as he also rebuilt his church at Worcester on the Norman model, albeit weeping at the passing of the old.[53]

In thus rehearsing all the evidence demonstrating that the origins of English feudalism lie in the Norman Conquest, we may revert at length to Maitland's point of feudal jurisdiction.[54] While, as we have seen, this is not amongst the unique fundamentals of feudal society, there is no doubt that it is a characteristic feature of the developed feudalism of the later eleventh century and thereafter, and while the Cloud of Unknowing descends upon the subject of private jurisdiction in pre-Conquest England,[55] most historians would agree that the honorial court, wherein the lord, by virtue of his lordship, exercises jurisdiction in civil pleas over the vassals of his honor, is an innovation in England as from 1066. Such jurisdiction in pleas of land is explicitly assumed, for example, in a well-known writ of Henry I (that well-known 'anti-feudal' monarch) touching the proper holding of the county, hundred and other local courts,[56] and the legal treatise called the *Leges Henrici Primi*, compiled in his reign, contains the most emphatic statement of the right of lords to jurisdiction over their tenants to be found in English history – 'Every lord may summon his man in order to do justice upon him in his court; and if the man is resident in the most remote manor of that honor of which he holds, he shall nevertheless go to the plea if his lord shall

---

[51] *Liber Eliensis*, 217; Doc. 37. Cf. the disturbance of monastic peace at Worcester in Wulfstan's time, according to William of Malmesbury's *Vita Wulfstani*, ed. R. R. Darlington, 55–6. Cf. also Doc. 35.

[52] *De Gestis Pontificum.* ed. Hamilton, 281. Doc. 34. Cf. *Vita Wulfstani*, 55.

[53] *De Gestis Pontificum*, 283; *Vita Wulfstani*, 52.

[54] Cf. above, p. 31.

[55] Cf. Stenton, *Anglo-Saxon England*, 485 – 'The origin of private justice is one of the unsolved problems of Anglo-Saxon history'.

[56] Stubbs, *Select Charters*, 122; A. J. Robertson, *Laws of the Kings of England from Edmund to Henry I*, 286–7; Doc. 53. Note the intensely feudal language.

summon him.'[57] Yet again it should not be supposed, as it often is, that in this respect especially feudalism detracts from royal authority; for the King is the greatest feudal lord of all, the whole of England is his honor, and by virtue of his feudal position he thus has, after 1066, an automatic jurisdiction over the most important magnates of the realm, his tenants-in-chief, his barons. It is this, combined with the sheer circumstances of the Conquest, the Norman tenurial revolution and the problems and pleas arising therefrom, which gives that great impetus to the expansion of royal justice, and hence the development of the Common Law, which is itself not the least important result of 1066.

We thus reach an end. The fundamentals of feudalism – the knight, vassalic commendation, the fief, the castle – are all of them absent from the indigenous society, whether Anglo-Saxon or Scandinavian, of pre-Conquest England, and all are increasingly manifest after 1066. The origins of English feudalism, therefore, are found in the Norman Conquest. Finally, if it be asked, as one's better students do ask, why it was – and, more pertinently, how it could have been – that England before the Conquest could have been so different from northern France, a mere twenty-five miles away beyond the Channel crossed by Duke William's invading fleet, the answer lies in the history, the different history, of this country. In Frankia, though the origins of some of the individual elements which will fuse into feudalism can be traced further back, the origins and formation of feudal society itself lie in the disintegration of the over-mighty Carolingian state in the ninth century,[58] through its own inherent weaknesses after the death of Charlemagne and the assaults upon it by the Vikings, the Muslims and the Magyars. Kingship is older than feudalism. In what will be France the collapse of central authority caused society painfully to reform itself on the basis of local, feudal lordship. But here we find the great paradox of English history. The result of the ninth century in England was not the collapse of royal authority but its expansion. Alfred of Wessex held out against the Danes and his successors reconquered the Danelaw to achieve, for the first time, a united country under a single monarchy. Defeat when it came eventually at the hands of Cnut was a national defeat, a change of dynasty and, to some extent, of ruling class, and led to no disintegration of the realm, no waning of royal power. England and France in the ninth and tenth centuries were set upon divergent courses, and in England the Old World, Germanic and pre-feudal, survived until 1066, when it went down before the New.

---

[57] 'Omni domino licet submonere hominem suum, ut ei sit ad rectum in curia sua: et si residens est ad remotius manerium ejusdem honoris unde tenet, ibit ad placitum, si dominus suus submoneat eum', Stubbs, Select Charters, 126; English Historical Documents, ii. 461. Doc. 63.

[58] Cf. above, pp. 25, 28.

PART 2: DOCUMENTS

Documents

THE documents which follow (though numbered consecutively throughout for reference purposes) have been arranged in the categories of the types of evidence available – (a) literary and narrative sources (b) charters, leases, writs, etc. (c) laws, custumals etc (d) surveys (e) artistic and archaeological – and within these categories in a roughly chronological order. An alternative arrangement by subjects (e.g. tenure, military organization, tactics) would lead to far too much overlap and repetition, as well as perhaps imposing a pre-conceived pattern upon the reader to an even greater degree than a selection of documents of this type is in any case likely to do. In every case reference is given to a reliable text of the document or extract in the original language, whether Latin or the vernacular 'Anglo-Saxon', for it cannot be too strongly stressed that no translation is an adequate substitute for the original, especially in this subject in this period when feudal terminology was itself in process of formation and evolution. Further, this is as true of Anglo-Saxon sources as it is of Latin, even though most of us are constrained to study the former in translation, and do so with less conscience and concern than we would the latter. In the headings to the following documents, however, such references are not always and on principle to the, as it were, ultimate in scholarly texts and editions (e.g. Liebermann for laws), but rather, where possible, to reliable texts and editions more readily available to the generality of students (e.g. that invaluable compendium, Stubbs' *Select Charters*). In addition, reference is given to existing translations where such are available, though this chiefly with a view to bibliography and further reading: such translations have by no means invariably been followed here, and therefore, though gladly acknowledging their help, I must hold myself responsible for any errors and infelicities which occur. The date of compilation of the source from which the documents or extracts are derived is given where appropriate, most usually where the source is not more or less contemporary with the events or facts it relates.

A. Literary and Narrative Sources

1. FROM Tacitus, *Germania* [AD 98] cc. 13–14. W. Stubbs, *Select Charters* (9th edition, Oxford, 1923), 62–3. Translation, H. Mattingly, *Tacitus on Britain and Germany* (Harmondsworth, 1948), 111–12.

Conspicuous ancestry or great services rendered by their fathers can win the rank of chief [*principis*] for youths still in their teens. They are attached to other chiefs who are more mature and approved, nor is it any shame to be seen thus in the ranks of companions [*comites*]. This war-band [*comitatus*] has even its different grades, as decided by the leader; there is great rivalry among the companions for the first place by the chief, and among the chiefs for the most numerous and courageous companions. Dignity and power alike consist in being always surrounded by a corps of chosen youths, giving honour in peace-time and security in war. Nor is it only in a man's own nation that he can win name and fame by the superior number and quality of his companions, but in neighbouring states as well . . . On the field of battle it is a disgrace to the chief to be surpassed in valour by his companions, to the companions not to equal the valour of their chief. Furthermore, it is a life-long infamy and shame to survive the chief and withdraw from the fight. To defend him, to protect him, even to ascribe to his glory their own exploits, is the essence of their sworn allegiance. The chief fights for victory, the companions for their chief.

2. FROM *Annales regni Francorum*, ed. F. Kurze, (Hanover, 1895), 14, 16. Quoted and translated, Ganshof, *Feudalism*, 26.[1]

[AD 757. The duke of Bavaria commends himself to the Frankish king, Pepin III.]
Tassilo, duke of the Bavarians, came there [to Compiègne] and commended himself into vassalage by his hands [*in vasatico se commendans per manus*]; he swore many and innumerable oaths, placing his hands on the relics of saints, and he promised fealty to King Pepin and to his sons the aforementioned lords Charles and Carloman, as by law a vassal [*vassus*] ought to do with uprightness and devotion, assuming the position a vassal ought to have in relation to his lords.

3. FROM Richer, *Histoire de France*, ed. Robert Latouche (with

[1] For a further, fuller and later description of vassalic commendation, see Doc. 39.

French translation; Paris, 1930), i. 104. Quoted and translated, Ganshof, *Feudalism*, 64.

[AD 927. William Longsword, duke of Normandy, commends himself to King Charles the Simple.]
He committed himself into the hands of the king in order to serve him [*regis manibus sese militaturum committit*], and promised him fealty and confirmed it with an oath.

4. FROM Anglo-Saxon Chronicle, C(D,E), under the year 1016. Ed., in translation only, Dorothy Whitelock and others, 96. Vernacular text, C. Plummer, *Two of the Saxon Chronicles Parallel*, (Oxford, 1892–9), i. 150–1.

Then King Edmund [Ironside] collected all his army for the fourth time, and crossed the Thames at Brentford, and went into Kent. And the Danish army fled before him with their horses into Sheppey. The king killed as many of them as he could overtake. . . .

5. FROM Anglo-Saxon Chronicle, D, under the year 1051. Ed. Whitelock, 117–18. Plummer, as above, i. 175.[2]

[Concerning the rebellion of earl Godwin and his sons on the occasion of the visit to king Edward by Eustace count of Boulogne.]
Then earl Godwine was indignant that such things should happen in his earldom, and he began to gather his people from all over his earldom, and earl Swein his son did the same all over his, and Harold his other son over all his. And they all assembled in Gloucestershire at Langtree, a great and innumerable force all ready to do battle against the king unless Eustace [count of Boulgone] were surrendered and his men handed over to them, as well as the Frenchmen who were in the castle [*castell*].

6. FROM Anglo-Saxon Chronicle, E, under the year 1051. Ed. Whitelock, 119. Plummer, as above, i. 173–4.

The foreigners then had built a castle [*castel*] in Herefordshire in earl Swein's province, and had inflicted every possible injury and insult upon the king's men in those parts.

7. FROM Anglo-Saxon Chronicle, E, under the year 1052. Ed. Whitelock, 125. Plummer, i. 180–1.[3]

[2] Cf. No. Doc. 15.
[3] Cf. No. 16.

[Earl Godwin and his sons return from exile and advance upon London where king Edward awaits them.]

Then bishop Stigand with the help of God went there, and the wise men both inside the city and without, and they decided that hostages should be arranged for on both sides. And so it was done. Then Archbishop Robert[4] found out about this, and the Frenchmen, so that they took horses and departed, some west to Pentecost's castle [*castele*], and some north to Robert's castle [*castele*].

8. FROM Anglo-Saxon Chronicle, C, under the year 1055. Ed. Whitelock, 130. Plummer, i. 185–6.[5]

And then they [earl Ælfgar and Gruffyd ap Llywelyn] gathered a large force with the Irishmen and with the Welsh, and earl Ralph gathered a large force against them at Hereford town, and there battle was joined. But before any spear had been thrown the English army fled because they were on horses. . . .

9. FROM Anglo-Saxon Chronicle, D, under the year 1066. Ed. Whitelock, 142–3. Plummer, i. 199.

Then count William came from Normandy to Pevensey on Michaelmas Eve, and as soon as they were able to move on they built a castle [*castel*] at Hastings [*Haestinga port*].

10. FROM Anglo-Saxon Chronicle, E, under the year 1066. Ed. Whitelock, 141–2. Plummer, i. 198.

. . . and William conquered this country, and came to Westminster, and archbishop Aldred consecrated him king, and people paid taxes to him, and gave him hostages and afterwards bought their lands.

11. FROM Anglo-Saxon Chronicle, D, under the year 1066 [=1067]. Ed. Whitelock 145. Plummer, i. 200.

[In the spring of 1067 king William returns to Normandy to celebrate his victory.]

And bishop Odo and earl William [fitz Osbern] stayed behind and built castles [*castelas*] far and wide throughout this country, and distressed the wretched folk, and always after that it grew much worse. May the end be good when God wills!

---

4 Robert of Jumièges.
5 Cf. No. 17.

12. FROM Anglo-Saxon Chronicle, D, under the year 1074. Ed. Whitelock, 156. Plummer, i. 210.

[Edgar Æthling leaves his exile in Scotland for the king in Normandy]. Then king Malcolm advised him [Edgar] to send overseas to king William and ask for his protection, and he did so; and the king granted it to him and sent for him. And again king Malcolm and Edgar's sister gave him and all his men immense treasure, and again very honourably sent him out of their jurisdiction. And the sheriff of York came to meet them at Durham and went all the way with them and had them provided with food and fodder at every castle [castelle] they came to, until they got overseas to the king.

13. FROM Anglo-Saxon Chronicle, E, under the year 1086. Ed. Whitelock, 162. Plummer, i. 217. Text and translation, Stubbs, Select Charters, 96.

After that he [William I] went about so that he came at Lammas [1 August] to Salisbury, and there came to him his councillors and all the land-owning men of any account from all over England, whose soever men they were, and all bowed down to him [ealle hi bugon to him] and were his men, and swore oaths of fealty [hold athas] to him that they would be faithful to him against all other men.

14. FROM Anglo-Saxon Chronicle, E, under the year 1087. Ed. Whitelock, 164. Plummer, i. 220.

[Concerning William the Conqueror.]
                He had castles [castelas] built
                And poor men hard oppressed.

15. FROM Florence of Worcester, Chronicon ex Chronicis, [early twelfth century], ed. B. Thorpe, (English Historical Society, London, 1848–9), i. 205–6. Translation, English Historical Documents, ii, ed. D. C. Douglas (London, 1959), 207.[6]

[1051, concerning the rebellion of earl Godwin and his sons]. Meanwhile Godwin and his sons with their forces entered Gloucestershire after the Nativity of St Mary and encamped at a place called Langtree. They sent messengers to the king at Gloucester demanding on threat of war count Eustace and his companions, together with the Normans and men of Boulogne, who held the fortress [castellum] on the cliff at Dover.

[6] Cf. Doc. 5.

16. FROM Florence of Worcester, i. 210. Translation, *English Historical Documents*, ii. 209.[7]

[1052, concerning the return of earl Godwin and his sons from exile and the flight of king Edward's 'Norman favourites'].

Next, Robert archbishop of Canterbury, William bishop of London, and Ulf bishop of Lincoln, escaping with their Normans only with difficulty crossed the sea: but William, on account of his goodness, was recalled after a short time and reinstated in his see. Osbern, surnamed Pentecost, however, and his companion Hugh gave up their castles [*castella*] and, being allowed by earl Leofric to pass through his earldom, went to Scotland and were received by Macbeth, the king of Scots.

17. FROM Florence of Worcester, i. 213. Translation, *English Historical Documents*, ii. 210.[8]

[1055] Against whom [i.e. earl Ælfgar and his Welsh ally, Gruffydd ap Llewelyn] earl Ralph 'the Timid', the son of king Edward's sister, raised an army, and coming up with them two miles from Hereford city[9] on 24 October, commanded the English to fight on horseback contrary to their custom: but as battle was about to be joined the earl was the first to flee with his French and Normans. Seeing this, the English followed the example of their leader and were pursued by almost all the enemy who slew four or five hundred of them and wounded many others.

18. The Song of Maldon, Translation, *English Historical Documents*, i, ed. D. Whitelock (London, 1955), 293–7. Vernacular text with translation, M. Ashdown, *English and Norse Documents* (Cambridge, 1930), 3–37, 72–90.

[The Battle of Maldon, in Essex, was fought on 10 or 11 August, 991].
Then he bade each warrior leave his horse, drive it afar and go forth on foot, and trust to his hands and to his good intent.

Then Offa's kinsman first perceived that the earl would suffer no faintness of heart; he let his loved hawk fly from his hand to the wood and advanced to the fight. By this it might be seen that the lad would not waver in the strife now that he had taken up his arms.

With him Eadric would help his lord, his chief in the fray. He advanced to war with spear in hand; as long as he might grasp his shield and broad sword, he kept his purpose firm. He made good his vow, now that the time had come for him to fight before his lord.

---

[7] Cf. Doc. 7.
[8] Cf. No. 8 from the Anglo-Saxon Chronicle.
[9] 'Worcester in error, *English Historical Documents*, ii. 210.

Then Brihtnoth began to array his men; he rode and gave counsel and taught his warriors how they should stand and keep their ground, bade them hold their shields aright, firm with their hands and fear not at all. When he had meetly arrayed his host, he alighted among the people where it pleased him best, where he knew his bodyguard to be most loyal.

Then the messenger of the Vikings stood on the bank, he called sternly, uttered words, boastfully speaking the seafarers' message to the earl, as he stood on the shore. 'Bold seamen have sent me to you, and bade me say, that it is for you to send treasure quickly in return for peace, and it will be better for you all that you buy off an attack with tribute, rather than that men so fierce as we should give you battle. There is no need that we destroy each other, if you are rich enough for this. In return for the gold we are ready to make a truce with you. If you who are richest determine to redeem your people, and to give to the seamen on their own terms wealth to win their friendship and make peace with us, we will betake us to our ships with the treasure, put to sea and keep faith with you.'

Brihtnoth lifted up his voice, grasped his shield and shook his supple spear, gave forth words, angry and resolute, and made him answer: 'Hear you, searover, what this folk says? For tribute they will give you spears, poisoned point and ancient sword, such war gear as will profit you little in battle. Messenger of the seamen, take back a message, say to your people a far less pleasing tale, how that there stands here with his troop an earl of unstained renown, who is ready to guard this realm, the home of Ethelred my lord, people and land; it is the heathen that shall fall in the battle. It seems to me too poor a thing that you should go with our treasure unfought to your ships, now that you have made your way thus far into our land. Not so easily shall you win tribute; peace must be made with point and edge, with grim battle-play, before we give tribute.'

Then he bade the warriors advance, bearing their shields, until they all stood on the river bank. Because of the water neither host might come to the other. There came the tide, flowing in after the ebb; the currents met and joined. All too long it seemed before they might clash their spears together. Thus in noble array they stood about Pante's stream, the flower of the East Saxons and the shipmen's host. None of them might harm another, unless a man should meet his death through a javelin's flight.

The tide went out, the seamen stood ready, many a Viking eager for war. Then the bulwark of heroes appointed a warrior, hardy in war, to hold the bridge, Wulfstan was his name, accounted valiant among his kin. It was he, Ceola's son, who with his javelin shot down the first man that was so hardy as to set foot upon the bridge. There with Wulfstan stood warriors unafraid, Ælfhere and Maccus, a dauntless pair; they had no thought of flight at the ford, but warded themselves stoutly against the foe, as long as they might wield their weapons. When the Vikings knew and saw full well that they had to deal with grim defenders of the bridge, the hateful strangers betook themselves to guile, craved leave to land, to pass over the ford and lead their men across. Then the earl, in his pride, began to give ground all too much to the hateful folk; Brihthelm's son called over the cold water (the warriors gave ear): 'Now is the way open before you; come quickly, men, to meet us in battle. God alone knows to whom it shall fall to hold the field.'

The wolves of slaughter pressed forward, they recked not for the water, that viking host; west over Pante, over the gleaming water they came with their bucklers, the seamen came to land with their linden shields.

There, ready to meet the foe, stood Brihtnoth and his men. He bade them form the war-hedge with their shields, and hold their ranks stoutly against the foe. The battle was now at hand, and the glory that comes in strife. Now was the time when those who were doomed should fall. Clamour arose; ravens went circling, the eagle greedy for carrion. There was a cry upon earth.

They let the spears, hard as files, fly from their hands, well-ground javelins. Bows were busy, point pierced shield; fierce was the rush of battle, warriors fell on either hand, men lay dead. Wulfmaer was wounded, he took his place among the slain; Brihtnoth's kinsman, his sister's son, was cruelly cut down with swords. Then was payment given to the vikings; I heard that Edward smote one fiercely with his blade, and spared not his stroke, so that the doomed warrior fell at his feet. For this his lord gave his chamberlain thanks when time allowed.

Thus the stout-hearted warriors held their ground in the fray. Eagerly they strove, those men at arms, who might be the first to take with his spear the life of some doomed man. The slain fell to the earth.

The men stood firm; Brihtnoth exhorted them, bade each warrior, who would win glory in fight against the Danes, to give his mind to war.

Then came one, strong in battle; he raised his weapon, his shield to defend him, and bore down upon the man; the earl, no less resolute, advanced against the 'churl'. Each had an evil intent toward the other. Then the pirate sent a southern spear, so that the lord of warriors was stricken. He pushed with his shield so that the shaft was splintered, and shivered the spear so that it sprang back again. The warrior was enraged; he pierced with his lance the proud viking who had given him the wound. The warrior was deft; he drove his spear through the young man's neck; his hand guided it so that it took the life of his deadly foe. Quickly he shot down another, so that his corselet burst asunder; he was wounded through his mail in the breast, a poisoned point pierced his heart. The earl was the more content; then the proud man laughed, and gave thanks to his Creator for the day's work that the Lord had granted him.

Then one of the warriors let a dart fly from his hand, so that it pierced all too deeply Ethelred's noble thegn. By his side stood a warrior not yet full grown, a boy in war. Right boldly he drew from the warrior the bloody spear, Wulfstan's son, Wulfmaer the young, and let the weapon, wondrous strong, speed back again; the point drove in so that he who had so cruelly pierced his lord lay dead on the ground. Then a man, all armed, approached the earl, with intent to bear off the warrior's treasure, his raiment and his rings and his well-decked sword. Then Brihtnoth drew his blade, broad and of burnished edge, and smote upon his mail. All too quickly one of the seamen checked his hand, crippling the arm of the earl. Then his golden-hilted sword fell to the earth; he could not use his hard blade nor wield a weapon. Yet still the white-haired warrior spoke as before, emboldened his men and bade the heroes press on. He could no longer now stand firm on his feet. The earl looked up to heaven and cried aloud: 'I thank thee, Ruler of Nations, for all the joys that I have met with in this world. Now I have most need, gracious Creator, that thou grant my spirit grace, that my soul may fare to thee, into they keeping, Lord of Angels, and pass in peace. It is my prayer to thee that fiends of hell may not entreat it shamefully.'

Then the heathen wretches cut him down, and both the warriors who stood near by, Ælfnoth and Wulfmaer, lay overthrown; they yielded their lives at their lord's side.

Then those who had no wish to be there turned from the battle. Odda's sons were first in the flight; Godric for one turned his back on war, forsook the hero who had given him many a steed. He leapt upon the horse that had been his lord's, on the trappings to which he had no right. With him his brothers both galloped away, Godwine and Godwig, they had no taste for war, but turned from the battle and made for the wood, fled to the fastness and saved their lives, and more men than was fitting at all, if they had but remembered all the favours that he had done them for their good. It was as Offa had told them on the field when he held a council, that many were speaking proudly there, who later would not stand firm in time of need.

Now was fallen the people's chief, Ethelred's earl. All the retainers saw how their lord lay dead. Then the proud thegns pressed on, hastened eagerly, those undaunted men. All desired one of two things, to lose their lives or to avenge the one they loved.

With these words Ælfric's son urged them to go forth, a warrior young in years, he lifted up his voice and spoke with courage. Ælfwine said: 'Remember the words that we uttered many a time over the mead, when on the bench, heroes in hall, we made our boast about hard strife. Now it may be proved which of us is bold! I will make known my lineage to all, how I was born in Mercia of a great race. Ealhhelm was my grandfather called, a wise ealdorman, happy in the world's goods. Thegns shall have no cause to reproach me among my people that I was ready to forsake this action, and seek my home, now that my lord lies low, cut down in battle. This is no common grief to me, he was both my kinsman and my lord.'

Then he advanced (his mind was set on revenge), till he pierced with his lance a seaman from among the host, so that the man lay on the earth, borne down with his weapon.

Then Offa began to exhort his comrades, his friends and companions, that they should press on. He lifted up his voice and shook his ashwood spear: 'Lo! Ælfwine, you have exhorted all us thegns in time of need. Now that our lord lies low, the earl on the ground, it is needful for us all that each warrior embolden the other to war, as long as he can keep and hold his weapon, hard blade, spear and trusty sword. Godric, Odda's cowardly son, has betrayed us all. Too many a man, when he rode on that horse, on that proud steed, deemed that it was our lord. So was our host divided on the field, the shield-wall broken. A curse upon his deed, in that he has put so many a man to flight!'

Leofsunu lifted up his voice and raised his shield, his buckler to defend him, and gave him answer: 'This I avow, that I will not flee a foot-space hence, but will press on and avenge my liege-lord in the fight. About Sturmer the steadfast heroes will have no need to reproach me now that my lord has fallen, that I made my way home, and turned from the battle, a lordless man. Rather shall weapon, spear-point and iron blade, be my end.' He pressed on wrathful and fought sternly, despising flight.

Dunhere spoke and shook his lance; a simple churl, he cried above them all, and bade each warrior avenge Brihtnoth: 'He that thinks to avenge his lord, his chief in the press, may not waver nor reck for his life.' Then they went forth, and took no thought for life; the retainers began to fight hardily, those fierce warriors. They prayed God that they might take vengeance for their lord, and work slaughter among their foes.

The hostage began to help them eagerly; he came of a stout Northumbrian kin, Æscferth was his name, Ecglaf's son. He did not flinch in the war-play, but urged forth the dart unceasingly. Now he shot upon a shield, now he hit his man; ever he dealt out wounds, as long as he could wield his weapons.

Still in the van stood Edward the Long, bold and eager; he spoke vaunting words, how that he would not flee a foot-space or turn back, now that his lord lay dead. He broke the shield-wall and fought against the warriors, until he had taken due vengeance upon the seamen for his lord. Then he himself lay among the slain.

So too did Æthelric, Sigebriht's brother, a noble companion, eager and impetuous, he fought right fiercely, and many another. They clove the hollow shield and defended themselves boldly. The buckler's edge burst and the corselet sang a fearful song.

Then Offa smote a seaman in the fight, so that he fell to the earth. Gadd's kinsman too was brought to the ground, Offa himself was quickly cut to pieces in the fray. Yet he had compassed what he had promised his chief, as he bandied vows with his generous lord in days gone by, that they should both ride home to the town unhurt or fall among the host, perish of wounds on the field. He lay, as befits a thegn, at his lord's side.

Then came a crashing of shields; seamen pressed on, enraged by war; the spear oft pierced the life-house of the doomed. Wigstan went forth, Thurstan's son, and fought against the men. Wighelm's child was the death of three in the press, before he himself lay among the slain.

That was a fierce encounter; warriors stood firm in the strife. Men were falling, worn out with their wounds the slain fell to the earth.

Oswold and Eadwold all the while, that pair of brothers, urged on the men; prayed their dear kinsmen to stand firm in the hour of need, and use their weapons in no weak fashion.

Brihtwold spoke and grasped his shield (he was an old companion); he shook his ash-wood spear and exhorted the men right boldly: 'Thoughts must be the braver, heart more valiant, courage the greater as our strength grows less. Here lies our lord, all cut down, the hero in the dust. Long may he mourn who thinks now to turn from the battle-play. I am old in years; I will not leave the field, but think to lie by my lord's side, by the man I held so dear.'

Soo too Godric, Æthelgar's son, emboldened them all to battle. Often he launched his javelin, his deadly spear, upon the vikings; thus he advanced in the forefront of the host; he hewed and laid low, until he too fell in the strife. It was not the same Godric that fled from the battle.

19. FROM Snorre Sturlason, *The Heimskringla or the Sagas of the Norse Kings*, ed. in translation, R. B. Anderson, iv (London, 1889), 39–49. Separate edition and translation (followed here) of *King Harold's Saga* extracted from the *Heimskringla* by Magnus Magnasson and Hermann Palsson (Harmondsworth, 1966), 144–54.

[Snorre lived from 1179–1241 and wrote the following account of the Battle of Stamford Bridge (fought on 25 September, 1066) in the early thirteenth century].

Chapter 86. At Stamford Bridge

Earl Tostig had travelled north from Flanders to join King Harald as soon as he arrived in England, and so the earl took part in all these battles.

And just as Earl Tostig had told Harald previously, a large number of Englishmen came and joined them; these were Earl Tostig's friends and kinsmen, and they added greatly to the strength of Harald's army.

After the battle which has just been described[10] most of the people in the surrounding district submitted to King Harald, but some fled.

King Harald now prepared to advance on the town of York, and assembled his army at Stamford Bridge; and since he had won such a great victory against powerful chieftains and a mighty army, all the inhabitants were too frightened to offer any resistance. So the townspeople decided to send a message to King Harald, offering to deliver themselves and the town into his power.

In accordance with this offer, King Harald marched on York with all his army on the Sunday. Just outside the town he held an assembly of his men, attended also by representatives of the townspeople. All the townspeople gave their allegiance to King Harald, and gave him as hostages the sons of all the leading men; Earl Tostig knew about everyone in the town.

In the evening, King Harald went back to his ships, delighted with his easy victory; it had been agreed to hold a meeting in the town early the next morning, at which King Harald was to appoint officials to rule the town and distribute titles and estates.

But that very same evening after sunset, King Harold Godwinsson of England arrived at York from the south with a huge army, and rode straight into the town with the full consent of all the townspeople. Then all the town's gates were closed and all the roads blocked, so that the news should not reach the Norwegians. The English army spent the night in the town.

Chapter 87. The armies meet

On Monday, when King Harald Sigurdsson had breakfasted, he ordered the trumpets to sound the order for disembarkation. He got the army ready and divided his forces, choosing which of them were to go with him and which were to stay behind: from each company two men were to go for every one that was left behind.

Earl Tostig prepared his troops for landing to go with King Harald; the men who were left behind to guard the ships were the king's son, Olaf, Earl Paul and Earl Erlend of Orkney, and Eystein Orri, the noblest of all the landed men and dearest to the king, to whom the king had promised his daughter Maria in marriage.

[12] I.e. Fulford.

The weather was exceptionally fine, with warm sunshine; so the troops left their armour behind and went ashore with only their shields, helmets, and spears, and girt with swords. A number of them also had bows and arrows. They were all feeling very carefree.

But as they approached the town they saw a large force riding to meet them. They could see the cloud of dust raised by the horses' hooves, and below it the gleam of handsome shields and white coats of mail. King Harald halted his troops and summoned Earl Tostig, and asked him what army this could be. Earl Tostig said he thought it was likely to be a hostile force, although it was also possible that these were some of his kinsmen seeking mercy and protection from the king in exchange for their faith and fealty. The king said they had better wait there and find out more about this army. They did so; and the closer the army came, the greater it grew, and their glittering weapons sparkled like a field of broken ice.

Chapter 88. Preparations.

King Harald Sigurdsson said, 'We must now think up a good and effective plan, for it is quite obvious that these are hostile troops; it must be the king himself'.

Earl Tostig replied, 'The first thing to do is to turn and head back to our ships as quickly as possible for the rest of our men and weapons. Then we will be in a stronger position to face them, or else we could let our ships protect us, for then the cavalry could not get at us'.

'I have another plan,' said King Harald. 'We shall send three brave warriors on the fastest horses we have, and let them ride with all speed to inform our men – and they will come to our help at once. The English will have a very hard fight of it before we accept defeat'.

The earl told the king to decide in this as in everything else, and added that it was by no means his own wish to flee.

So King Harald ordered his banner, 'Land-Waster', to be raised; it was carried by a man called Fridrek.

Chapter 89. Battle array

King Harald now drew up his army, and formed a long and rather thin line; the wings were bent back until they met, thus forming a wide circle of even depth all the way round, with shields overlapping in front and above. The king himself was inside the circle with his standard and his own retinue of hand-picked men.

Earl Tostig was also stationed inside the circle with his own company, and he had his own banner.

The army was formed up in this way because King Harald knew that cavalry always attacked in small detachments and then wheeled away at once. The king said that his own retinue and Earl Tostig's company would make sorties to wherever the need was greatest: 'Our archers are also to stay here with us. Those in the front rank are to set their spear-shafts into the ground and turn the points towards the riders' breasts when they charge us; and those immediately behind are to set their spears against the horses' chests.'

Chapter 90. Harold Godwinsson

King Harold Godwinsson had arrived there with a vast army, both cavalry and infantry.

King Harald of Norway now rode round his lines to inspect the forma-tion. He was riding a black horse with a blaze, which stumbled under him, and threw him off forwards. The king jumped quickly to his feet and said, 'A fall is fortune on the way.'

Then King Harold of England said to some Norwegians who were with him, 'Did you recognize that big man who fell off his horse, the man with the blue tunic and the beautiful helmet?'

'That was the king himself,' they said.

The King of England said, 'What a big, formidable-looking man he is: let us hope his good luck has now run out.'

Chapter 91. 'Seven feet of ground'

Twenty horsemen from the English king's company of Housecarls came riding up to the Norwegian lines; they were all wearing coats of mail, and so were their horses.

One of the riders said, 'Is Earl Tostig here in this army?'

Tostig replied, 'There is no denying it – you can find him here.'

Another of the riders said, 'Your brother King Harold sends you his greetings, and this message to say you can have peace and the whole of Northumbria as well. Rather than have you refuse to join him, he is prepared to give you one third of all his kingdom.'

The earl answered. 'This is very different from all the hostility and humiliation he offered me last winter. If this offer had been made then, many a man who is now dead would still be alive, and England would now be in a better state. But if I accept this offer now, what will he offer King Harald Sigurdsson for all his effort?'

The rider said, 'King Harold has already declared how much of England he is prepared to grant him: seven feet of ground or as much more as he is taller than other men.'

Earl Tostig said, 'Go now and tell King Harold to make ready for battle. The Norwegians will never be able to say that Earl Tostig abandoned King Harald Sigurdsson to join his enemies when he came west to fight in England. We are united in our aim: either to die with honour, or else conquer England.'

The horsemen now rode back.

Then King Harald Sigurdsson asked, 'Who was that man who spoke so well?.

'That was King Harold Godwinsson', replied Tostig.

King Harald Sigurdsson said, 'I should have been told much sooner. These men came so close to our lines that this Harold should not have lived to tell of the deaths of our men.'

'It is is quite true, sire,' said Earl Tostig, 'that the king acted unwarily, and what you say could well have happened. But I realized that he wanted to offer me my life and great dominions, and I would have been his murderer if I had revealed his identity. I would rather that he were my killer than I his.'

King Harald Sigurdsson said to his men, 'What a little man that was; but he stood proudly in his stirrups.'

It is said that King Harald Sigurdsson composed this stanza at the time:

> We go forward
> Into battle
> Without armour
> Against blue blades.
> Helmets glitter.
> My coat of mail
> And all our armour
> Are at the ships.

His coat of mail was called Emma; it was so long that it reached below his knee, and so strong that no weapon could pierce it. King Harald then said, 'That was a poor verse; I shall have to make a better one.' He composed another stanza:

> We never kneel in battle
> Before the storm of weapons
> And crouch behind our shields;
> So the noble lady told me.
> She told me once to carry
> My head always high in battle
> Where swords seek to shatter
> The skulls of doomed warriors.

Then the poet Thjodolf said:

> Though Harald himself should fall,
> Never shall I abandon

The king's young heirs;
God's will be done.
The sun never shone
On more promising princes;
The two young eaglets
Would soon avenge their father.

Chapter 92. The Battle of Stamford Bridge.

Now the battle began. The English made a cavalry charge on the Norwegians, who met it without flinching. It was no easy matter for the English to ride against the Norwegians because of their arrows, so they rode around them in a circle. There was only skirmishing to begin with, so long as the Norwegians kept their formation. The English cavalry kept charging them and falling back at once when they could make no headway.

The Norwegians observed this, and thought the enemy assaults rather half-hearted; so they launched an attack themselves on the retreating cavalry. But as soon as they had broken their shield-wall, the English rode down on them from all sides, showering spears and arrows on them.

When King Harald Sigurdsson saw this, he led a charge into the thickest of the fighting. The battle became very fierce, and great numbers were killed on both sides. King Harald Sigurdsson now fell into such a fury of battle that he rushed forward ahead of his troops, fighting two-handed. Neither helmets nor coats of mail could withstand him, and everyone in his path gave way before him. It looked then as if the English were on the point of being routed. In the words of Arnor the Earls'-Poet:

Norway's king had nothing
To shield his breast in battle;
And yet his war-seasoned
Heart never wavered.
Norway's warriors were watching
The blood-dripping sword
Of their courageous leader
Cutting down his enemies.

But now King Harald Sigurdsson was struck in the throat by an arrow, and this was his death-wound. He fell, and with him fell all those who had advanced with him, except those who retreated with the royal standard.

The battle still raged fiercely, and Earl Tostig was now fighting under the royal standard. Both sides drew back to form up again, and there was a long lull in the fighting. Then the poet Thjodolf said:

Disaster has befallen us;
I say the army has been duped.
There was no cause for Harald
To bring his forces westward.
Mighty Harald is fallen
And we are all imperilled;
Norway's renowned leader
Has lost his life in England.

Before the fighting was resumed, Harold Godwinsson offered quarter to his brother Tostig and all the surviving Norwegians. But the Norwegians shouted back with one voice that every one of them would rather die than accept quarter from the English; they roared their war-cry, and the battle started again. In the words of Arnor the Earls'-Poet:

It was an evil moment
When Norway's king lay fallen;
Gold-inlaid weapons
Brought death to Norway's leader.
All King Harald's warriors
Preferred to die beside him,
Sharing their brave king's fate,
Rather than beg for mercy.

Chapter 93. Orri's battle

At this point Eystein Orri arrived from the ships with all the men he had; they were wearing coats of mail. Eystein took King Harald's banner, 'Land-Waster', and the fighting began for the third time, more fiercely than ever. The English fell in great numbers, and once again were on the point of being routed. This stage of the fighting was called Orri's Battle.

Eystein and his men had run all the way from the ships so hard that they were tired out and almost unable to fight before they arrived on the scene. But then they fell into such a battle fury that they did not bother to protect themselves as long as they could still stand on their feet. Eventually they threw off their coats of mail, and after that it was easy for the English to land blows on them; but some of the Norwegians collapsed from exhaustion and died unwounded. Nearly all the leading Norwegians were killed there.

It was now late in the afternoon. As was to be expected not all reacted in the same way; a number of them fled, and others were lucky enough to survive in different ways. It had grown dark before the carnage ended.

H

20. FROM *The Life of Herluin, Abbot of Bec* by Gilbert Crispin, printed in J. Armitage Robinson, *Gilbert Crispin Abbot of Westminster* (Cambridge, 1911), 87–91.[11]

As memorable military achievements are put down in writing for the inspiration of posterity, and lauded according to the character and abilities of the author, we have no excuse for not recording, to the glory of divine virtue and as a pattern of mighty faith in God, the deeds performed in our memory in the service [*satellitio*] of Christ by the venerable abbot Herluin of Bec. And this may be put first as furnishing some proof of his virtue, that, when the world was looking with favour upon his every wish, he totally rejected it, at an age when others are thrusting themselves the more insistently upon a world that spurns them, and this in a country where for a knight, as yet unscathed, to lay down his arms to become a monk was regarded as a wonder.

His father traced his origins from the Danes who first occupied Normandy; his mother was closely related to the dukes of Flanders. The one was called Ansgot, the other Helois. Gilbert count of Brionne,[12] a grandson of Richard I, duke of Normandy, through his son count Godfrey, had charge of his upbringing, and treated him with the utmost favour among all the leading men of his court. He had great aptitude for the pursuit of arms and devoted himself to it with no less enthusiasm. All the chief families of Normandy held him in high esteem, and extolled his knightly prowess and physical accomplishments. He disregarded anything dishonourable, but concentrated all his efforts upon those honourable affairs which are highly valued at courts. He was eager to be outstanding among his fellow knights both in the household and the field, and thus he had not only won singular favour with his lord, but had acquired a reputation and a ready welcome with Robert, duke of the whole country,[13] and with the lords of other regions. We may pass over such other things as he achieved in seeking a name in the world, but we should not omit the following, in illustration of his strength of mind, the constancy of his faith, and his confidence in arms.

Resenting on one occasion an injury done him by his lord, who was withholding from him the rewards of his service, Herluin betook himself far from his displeasure. At about this time, this same Count Gilbert had suffered injuries from certain of the most powerful men of Normandy, and, wishing to make it known that his injuries would be avenged, he assembled a large force of knights. He was a man of fierce spirit and great power, and as the kinsman of such great dukes was hungry for a lofty reputation. In order to advertise his strength, he

[11] I am very much indebted to my colleague Miss Diana Barron for most of the translation of this passage.
[12] Ancestor of the house of Clare in England, *d.c.* 1040.
[13] i.e. Robert the Magnificent, duke of Normany, 1027–35.

advised his enemies by messengers of what he proposed to do and when, not just beforehand but several days in advance. At the appointed time, therefore, both sides were preparing for a war that could neither be waged without great bloodshed on both sides, nor avoided without loss of honour.

When the valiant man of whom we have undertaken to write heard of this, he forgot his injuries forthwith, and, taking with him twenty chosen knights, set out for the day of battle, not indeed to join his lord but remaining separate from his forces. By exposing the safety of himself and his men, and by risking death, he was seeking to make good the solemn pledge of his fealty; he asked for nothing from the count in return. The facts speak for themselves, and show clearly what manner of man he was. We address this example not to those who are unmanned by fear and desert from battle to the ruin of others, but to those who are induced by greed to seek the death of their lords and the destruction of their country. Nor do we bring it forward so much as a justification for military glory as for the sake of keeping faith.

The count [dux] was leading his forces over the flank of a high mountain when he noticed twenty armed men following some way behind on the plain. Fearing hostile intent, he detailed some of his men to investigate. They approached Herluin's troop, learnt his purpose, and, applauding his magnanimity, reported back to the count [duci]. Marvelling that he should receive such service in return for injury, the count immediately readmitted Herluin to his side and restored to him with enhanced favour everything that had been his. At dawn of the following day, envoys of the aforesaid Robert, duke of the province, arrived in time to scotch the imminent conflict, calling upon the parties in the name of right and sworn fealty to desist from war and to await the decision of his court instead of the judgement of battle. . . .

Herluin, thus happily placed, was more than thirty-seven years old when at long last his mind began to be inflamed by the divine love, so that his love of the world grew lukewarm and with the passing days gradually cooled, as he turned the eyes of his heart from external things on to himself. He went frequently to church, prayed with great devotion and often prostrated himself in tears. Forgetful of all trivialities, he was seen less frequently in court. He was held there only by his efforts to obtain his lands as well as himself for God, and this he finally achieved, extracting them from his lord by dint of great perseverance. Often he would spend the night praying in churches and in the morning be the first to arrive at his lord's table. As he did not want to practice abstinence amongst his companions, he absented himself on various contrived pretexts, often passing the whole day in fasting. He did not devote himself as before to arms or physical pursuits, in itself sufficient indication of the conflict in his mind, which he had hitherto been careful to conceal. To relinquish knighthood [*militia*] and all other wordly affairs was the sum of his desire. Where he was to go and what manner of life he was to adopt he did not know. There was scarcely any guide or pointer to the right path in the Normandy of that time. Priests and bishops were regularly married and bore arms like laymen; all lived according to the old Danish customs. But just as the spirit bloweth where it listeth, so it teaches everything to him whom it has anointed. Thus renouncing arms, dressed in cheap clothing, his beard and hair uncut, Herluin long remained among the other members of the household with that one intention of which we have spoken – he was the Hebrew preparing to leave Egypt ... Still he sat gladly beside his lord at table, and surrounded by all kinds of dishes and his roistering companions, he ate coarse bread and water. They all laughed at him and thought that all he did was madness. His lord and his followers could do nothing by threats, slights or promises, in all their efforts to divert him from his purpose. The man who had once been highly esteemed by all frequently went on missions to other courts mounted on an ass, an object of sorrow or derision to different people for his mode of transport, and indeed for the cheapness of his services,[14] for he was afraid of becoming entangled in the world, nor wished any longer to ride horses, serving on the back of an ass the lord from whom he was unwilling to depart without permission. And as he was not at all ashamed to humble himself for the sake of God, so God was not ashamed of him and rendered unto him even upon earth a still greater reward.

Count Gilbert was seeking to achieve the downfall of one of his compatriots, and charged Herluin with a mission to Robert prince of Normandy, whose responsibility it was to deal with anything arising from this matter. But the man [*vir*] of peace totally refused to act as agent in a plot against anyone. His lord persisted in his command, urging and threatening that his intimate vassal [*homo sibi intimus*] should bear the word of his council to his [the count's] own lord. So it came about that the knight, faced with the choice, had to show whether he preferred to serve his earthly or his heavenly lord; and, as the purposes of the heavenly lord demanded, he straightway broke the cord which held him to the service of the earthly lord: he washed his hands of the assignment and left the court. A few days later count Gilbert went to [*i.e.* the ducal] court, not doubting that Herluin had preceded him, and desiring to hear the duke's reply. When he learnt that the business had not been conveyed to him, he raged against the man to whom he had entrusted it, and ordered that everything belonging to him and his dependants should be confiscated. At once all Herluin's possessions were seized, which concerned him not at all; but his poor dependants were also despoiled, which caused him great concern. Impelled

[14] *servitiorum quidem gratiositate?*

therefore by their grief and their complaints he returned after a few days to his lord, not on his own behalf but as a suppliant for the innocent. The case was brought before the whole court and vigorously debated. The charges were laid, and Herluin was able to clear himself of them, giving humble but adequate reasons . . . 'Let everything that I have received from here be taken away', he said, 'but let the poor, who have done nothing to deserve your wrath, have their belongings back.' His lord who was greatly influenced by the pride of earthly rank, was moved to pity. Taking Herluin aside, he probed into his change of heart and his intentions. Herluin replied to him with few words but with many tears. 'Through loving the world and obeying you, I have hitherto too much neglected God and my own self. Concentrating entirely on tending the body I have done nothing for the instruction of my soul; wherefore I beg you, if ever I have deserved well of you, that I be permitted to spend the rest of my life in a monastery, preserving your love for me. Give my possessions along with me myself to God.'

Thus ended these long deliberations. Moved to tears, the count could no longer bear to hear him speak, and hastened into his chamber. He had a great deal of human feeling for this his knight, just as Herluin had for him, his lord. . . . At length [the count] granted to his beloved vassal [cliens] the desired release of himself and of all his possessions. Him whom he had hitherto loved as a good retainer, he now began to love as a lord and to obey him gladly. He kept Herluin with him most honourably for several days, and restored to him all his rightful honours. He made over to his lordship [ditio] and service everything that his brothers, born to equal dignity with him, held in right of their father; for he had acquired a higher and truer nobility than his brothers, and it did not seem inappropriate or unjust that the patrimony should be legally subjected to him.

Herluin at once began to erect in the place called Bonneville a building for the service of God, which although not small, was soon completed. He not only directed the work, but himself carried it out, digging up the earth, emptying trenches, carrying stone and sand and lime on his shoulders and himself placing them in position in the wall. At times when the others were absent, he would assemble the materials needed for the work, banishing idleness from every part of the day. True humility now made him as willing to bear any labour for God's sake as puffed-up vanity had once made him fastidious. He ate once a day, except on fast days; his food was not dainty and there was not much of it. His work ended with the day and because there was no other time he spent almost the whole night learning his psalter. With joyfulness the new esquire of Christ [tiro Christi] was trained by these exercises.

21. FROM William of Jumièges, *Gesta Normannorum Ducum*, ed.
J. Marx, (Rouen and Paris, 1914), 115–16.

[Concerning the minority of William the Bastard in Normandy, who
succeeded to a disputed succession in the duchy in 1035 at the age of 7].
In his early youth, many of the Normans, renouncing their fealty to
him, having raised earthworks [*erectis aggeribus*][15] in many places,
constructed for themselves the safest castles [*munitiones*]. When they
felt themselves thus sufficiently secure, a number of them at once
rebelled, stirred up sedition, and inflicted cruel destruction upon the
country.

22. FROM William of Jumièges, 123.

[Concerning duke William's victory at Val-ès-Dunes in 1047, which
marked his triumph in the duchy and the end of the troubles of his
minority].
The king[16] with the duke, unperturbed by the violent attack [of the
rebel forces], gave battle with a counter-charge of knights [*militum*], and
inflicted such slaughter upon them that those not cut down by the sword
were drowned as panic-stricken fugitives in the river Orne. A happy
battle indeed which in a single day brought about the collapse of so
many castles [*castella*] and dens[17] of evil deeds.

23. FROM William of Jumièges, 134.

[Concerning the Norman invasion of England in 1066].
Duke William therefore . . . seeing Harold daily grow in strength,
rapidly built a fleet of three thousand vessels and anchored it at St.
Valery in Ponthieu, loaded with fine horses and splendid warriors, with
hauberks and helmets. Thence with a following wind, sails spread aloft,
he crossed the sea to a landfall at Pevensey where he at once raised a
strongly fortified castle [*firmissimo vallo castrum condidit*]. Leaving a
garrison of knights [*milites*] in this, he moved on swiftly to Hastings
where he rapidly raised another.

24. FROM William of Poitiers, *Histoire de Guillaume le Conquérant*,
ed. R. Foreville (with French translation; Paris, 1962), 14–20.

[15] It would be quite legitimate to translate *agger* as 'mound', the root
meaning of the word (used here with *erigere*, to erect, raise up), in which case the
passage would have direct bearing on the current archaeological debate concerning the origin of Norman mottes, i.e. whether they are pre- or post-Conquest.
[16] i.e. Henry I of France, duke William's ally on this occasion.
[17] The word used is *domicilia*, i.e. residences, dwellings, thus showing the true
nature of the feudal castle as a fortified residence.

[Concerning the rebellion of 1047 against duke William in Normandy, the battle of Val-ès-Dunes and its aftermath].

The man who took the lead in this madness was Guy, son of Reginald count of Burgundy, who held the formidable castles [*castra*] of Brionne and Vernon by the duke's gift and had been brought up since boyhood in the duke's household. He coveted either the duchy itself or the best part of it. He associated with him in his evil conspiracy Nigel *vicomte* of Coutances, Ranulf *vicomte* of Bayeux, and Haimo surnamed *Dentatus* [the toothed], and other magnates. . . .

. . . Little by little this perjured conspiracy grew in strength until they directly challenged their lord by open war at Val-ès-Dunes . . . [The duke attacked and] instilled panic by the slaughter he inflicted, so that the heart went out of his enemies and their arms lost their strength. Flight became their one intent. He pursued them for some miles chastising them unmercifully. Many met their end in attempting difficult roads and bye-ways. Others were crushed to death in the headlong flight along the plain. Not a few were drowned, riders and horses alike, in the waters of the Orne. Henry king of France was present at this battle, aiding the cause of victory. Great indeed were the fruits of this battle of a single day, worthy to be commemorated by future ages, for it proclaimed a dire warning, it bowed necks too proud to the yoke, it cast down by the force of victory innumerable castles [*castella*], the fortresses of crime, and for long abolished in our country intestine wars.

[*An account of the successful (though in fact very prolonged) siege of Guy of Burgundy's castle at Brionne follows*] – This castle [*oppidum*], both by the manner of its construction and the nature of the site, seemed impregnable. For in addition to the other fortifications which the needs of war require, it has a stone-built hall serving the defenders as a keep [*arx*],[18] and about it the impatient waters of the river Risle flow without any ford. . . .[19]

. . . The Normans once vanquished all submitted to their lord and many gave hostages [*i.e.* of good faith]. Then at his command they immediately and completely demolished the castles [*munitiones*] they had constructed in their seditious zeal.

25. FROM William of Poitiers, 102–4.

[Concerning Harold's oath to William in *c*.1064].

At a council assembled at Bonneville, Harold swore fealty [*fidelitatem*

---

[18] The passage, of considerable interest as describing both an early stone castle and an early stone *donjon* or keep in pre-Conquest Normandy, is badly mistranslated by Foreville, p. 19.

[19] The present castle is sited on a hill above the town: this was evidently on an island in the river.

. . . *juravit*] to him [William] according to the sacred rite of Christians. And as the most trustworthy and distinguished men, witnesses at the time and with utter probity, have stated, to the main article of the oath he made, of his own free-will, these distinct additions:[20] that in the court of his lord, king Edward, he would be duke William's representative [*vicarius*] as long as the king should live; that he would use all his influence and resources so that the English kingdom after the death of Edward should be firmly established in the hand of the duke; that meanwhile he would hand over to the keeping of William's knights [*militum*] the castle [*castrum*] of Dover, fortified at his own cost and effort; also that he would similarly hand over, amply provided with supplies, other castles [*castra*] in various parts of the land where the duke should order them to be fortified. Before the oath, and at his request, the duke gave him, now his vassal by homage,[21] all his [Harold's] lands and power.

26. FROM William of Poitiers, 168.

[Concerning the Norman invasion of England, 1066].
Joyfully the Normans, having gained the shore, occupied first Pevensey, where they raised a castle [*munitio*], and then Hastings, where they raised another, each to serve as a defence both for themselves and for their ships.

27. FROM William of Poitiers, 184–204. Translation, *English Historical Documents*, ii. 225–9.

[The Battle of Hastings, Saturday, 14 October 1066].
This is the good order in which he [duke William] advanced, with the banner which the Pope had sent in the van. He placed infantry in front armed with bows and crossbows,[22] and in the second line also infantry more heavily armed with mail tunics [*loricatos*]; in the rear the squadrons of mounted knights [*equitum*], with himself in the centre with the élite force, so that he could direct everything by hand and voice. If any writer of Antiquity had described the army of Harold, he would have told how at his passage the rivers were drained and the forests levelled. For from all over the country vast forces of English had assembled. Some were drawn by love for Harold and all by love for their country, which they wished, though misguidedly, to defend against strangers. The land of

---

[20] *in serie summa sacramenti libens ipse haec distinxit.*

[21] *jam satelliti suo accepto per manus* – a clear reference to the act of homage by the *immixtio manuum*, distinct from the oath of fealty. To these two elements of vassalic commendation, investiture is added with the grant by the duke to Harold of the latter's lands.

[22] *Lit.* 'armed with arrows and crossbows' – *sagittis armatos et balistis.*

the Danes, their kith and kin, had sent them abundant help. Yet not
daring to fight on equal terms with William, whom they feared more
than the king of Norway,[23] they took up position on higher ground, on a
hill by the forest through which they had just come. At once abandoning
the aid of horses, they all drew themselves up on foot in very close order
indeed. The duke and his army, nothing daunted by the hard-going,
slowly advanced up the steep slope.

The terrible sound of trumpets on both sides announced the opening
of the battle. The eager courage of the Normans gave them the first
strike, just as when attornies meet in a trial for theft the prosecuting
counsel speaks first. So the Norman foot, coming in close, provoked the
English, raining wounds and death upon them with their missiles. They,
on the other hand, valiantly resisted, each according to his ability. They
threw spears and weapons of every kind, murderous axes and stones
tied to sticks. By these means you would have thought to see our men
overwhelmed as though by a deadly mass. And so the knights [equites]
came up in support, and those who were last became first. Spurning to
fight at long range, they challenged the event with their swords. Even
the war-cries of the Normans on the one side and the barbarians on the
other were drowned by the clash of arms and the groans of the dying.
Thus for some time the fight was waged with the utmost vigour on both
sides. The English were greatly helped by the advantage of the high
ground which they, in the closest array, could hold on the defensive;
also by their great number and massed strength; and further by their
weapons which could easily find a way through shields and other
defences. Thus they vigorously resisted or repulsed those who bravely
attacked them at close quarters with the sword. They even wounded
those who hurled javelins at them from a distance. Terrified by this
ferocity, behold! the foot-soldiers and also the Breton knights [equites],
together with all the auxiliaries on the left wing, are driven back. Almost
the whole ducal army falls away – though this may be said without dis-
paragement of the invincible Norman race. The army of imperial Rome,
containing the cohorts of kings, accustomed to victory by land and sea,
fled at times when it knew or thought its leader to be slain. The Normans
now believed their duke and leader had fallen. Their retreat was not
thus an occasion of shameful flight but of grief, for he was their whole
support.

The duke, therefore, seeing a large part of the enemy line launching
itself forward in pursuit of his retreating troops, galloped up in front of
them, shouting and brandishing his lance. Removing his helmet to bare
his head, he cried: 'Look at me. I am alive, and, by God's help, I shall
win. What madness puts you to flight? Where do you think you can go?
Those you could slaughter like cattle are driving and killing you. You

23 I.e. Harold Hardrada, whom they had just defeated at Stamford Bridge.

are deserting victory and everlasting honour; you are running away to destruction and everlasting shame. And by flight not one of you will avoid death.' At this, they recovered their morale. He himself was the first to charge forward, sword flashing, cutting down the foe who deserved death as rebels to him, their king. The Normans, enflamed, surrounded some thousands of those who had pursued them, and annihilated them in an instant, not one of them surviving.

Thus encouraged they renewed their attack upon the vast army which in spite of heavy losses seemed no less. The English, full of confidence, fought with all their might, determined above all to prevent any breach from being opened in their ranks. They were so densely massed that the dead could scarcely fall. However, breaches were cut in several places by the swords of the most redoubtable knights [*milites*]. They were closely followed up by the men of Maine and Aquitaine, the French, the Bretons, but above all by the Normans with courage beyond compare. A certain Norman esquire,[24] Robert, son of Roger de Beaumont and nephew and heir, through his mother, Adeline, of Hugh, count of Meulan, having that day his first experience of battle, bore himself in a way worthy of eternal praise, with great courage victoriously attacking at the head of the troop [*legio*] which he commanded on the right wing. But we have not the ability, nor is it our purpose, to relate as they deserve the feats of arms of individuals. The most accomplished and prolific writer, who had been an eye-witness of that battle, would find difficulty in describing each and every one. For our part we must now make haste so that, having reached the end of the fame of count William,[25] we may write of the glory of king William.

The Normans and their allied troops, realizing that they could not overcome an enemy so numerous and standing so firm without great loss to themselves, retreated, deliberately feigning flight [*terga dederunt, fugam ex industria simulantes*]. They remembered how a little while before flight had been the occasion of success. The barbarians exulted with the hope of victory. Exhorting each other with triumphant shouts they poured scorn upon our men and boasted that they would all be destroyed then and there. As before, some thousands of them were bold enough to launch themselves as if on wings after those they thought to be fleeing. The Normans, suddenly wheeling their horses about, cut them off, surrounded them, and slew them on all sides, leaving not one alive.

Twice they used the same stratagem to the same effect, and then attacked more furiously than ever the remaining enemy, still a formid-

---

[24] *Tiro*, a young man serving the apprenticeship of knighthood.

[25] I.e. duke William. The dukes of Normandy down to 1066 and beyond often described themselves, and were described, as 'count', either 'of the Normans' or of Rouen'.

able force and extremely difficult to surround. It was now a strange kind of battle, one side attacking with all mobility, the other enduring, as though rooted to the soil. The English began to weaken, and as if confessing their guilt by their submission, suffered the punishment. The Normans shot, smote and pierced: it seemed as if more movement was caused by the falling dead than by the living. Those only wounded could not withdraw, but died in the press of their companions. Thus Fortune sped to accomplish William's triumph.

There were present at this engagement Eustace, count of Boulogne; William, son of count Richard of Evreux; Geoffrey, son of Rotrou, count of Mortagne; William fitz Osbern; Aimeri, vicomte de Thouars; Walter Giffard; Hugh de Montfort: Ralph de Tosny; Hugh de Grandmesnil; William of Warenne; and many others famed in knightly renown and whose names should be recorded in the annals of history amongst the most celebrated warriors. William, however, their leader, so much excelled them all in bravery as in military skill that he may be held the equal or superior of those ancient leaders of the Greeks and Romans so much praised in books. He was a noble general, turning back the retreat, inspiring courage, sharing danger, more often commanding men to follow him than urging them on from the rear. It is very clear that his own surpassing courage and daring set the example to his followers. Not a few of the enemy, though unwounded, lost heart at the mere sight of this admirable and terrible knight [*eques*]. Three horses were killed under him. Three times he leapt to his feet undaunted and swiftly avenged the death of his steed. Then one could see his agility, his strength of both body and spirit. Shields, helmets, hauberks were riven by his furious and flashing blade, while yet other assailants were clouted by his own shield. His knights [*milites*] marvelled to see him a foot-soldier [*peditem*], and many, stricken with wounds, were given new heart. Not a few, from whom strength was ebbing with their blood, leant upon their shields to fight manfully on, while others, who could do no more, with hands and voice urged on their companions to follow the duke without fear, and not let victory slip from their grasp. He himself was the help and saviour of many.

[*There follows a paragraph in which William is compared with various classical heroes, and the author laments his incapacity to do justice to his theme*].

Now as the day declined the English army realized beyond doubt that they could no longer stand against the Normans. They knew that they were reduced by heavy losses; that the king himself, with his brothers and many magnates of the realm had fallen; that those who still stood were almost drained of strength; that they could expect no help. They saw the Normans not much diminished by casualties, threatening them more keenly than in the beginning, as if they had found new strength in the fight; they saw that fury of the duke who spared no one who resisted him; they saw that courage which could only find rest in victory. They therefore turned to flight and made off as soon as they got the chance, some on looted horses, many on foot; some along the roads, many across country. Those who struggled but on rising lacked the strength to flee lay in their own blood. The sheer will to survive gave strength to others. Many left their corpses in the depths of forests, many collapsed in the path of their pursuers along the way. The Normans, though not knowing the terrain, pursued them keenly, slaughtering the guilty fugitives and bringing matters to a fitting end, while the hooves of the horses exacted punishment from the dead as they were ridden over.

[*There follows a paragraph describing the incident of the 'Malfosse', where some of the fleeing English made a last stand, the pursuing knights suffered losses in the broken countryside, count Eustace of Boulogne, withdrawing and counselling withdrawal, was wounded, and the intrepid duke further distinguished himself though armed only with the stump of his broken lance.*][26]

His victory thus completed, [the duke] returned to the field of battle to inspect the carnage, which he could not look upon without sorrow although wrought upon rebels, and although to slay a tyrant is meet and right and worthy. Far and wide the ground was strewn with the flower of the English nobility and youth, soiled in blood. Close by the king two of his brothers were found, and he, lacking now in all dignity, was recognized only by certain marks, not by his face. He was borne to the duke's camp and committed for burial to William Malet, not to his mother who offered for the body of her beloved son its weight in gold. . . .

28. FROM William of Poitiers, 210–12. Translation, *English Historical Documents*, ii. 229.

[The morrow of Hastings].
Having buried his dead, and arranged for the custody of Hastings under a vigorous constable [*praefectus*], he [William] proceeded to Romney. . . . Thence he marched upon Dover, where he had heard that a great concourse of people had gathered, so that the place seemed impregnable. At his approach the English were daunted and lost confidence both in the natural and fortified strength of the position and in their own numbers. That fortress [*castellum*] is sited on a cliff beside the sea, which, naturally steep and everywhere improved in this respect by the work of man, rises sheer like a wall, as high as an arrow can be shot, on that side which is washed by the waters of the ocean. . . . The fortress [*castrum*]

---

[26] *Cum parte haste.*

taken, he spent eight days adding to it those fortifications which it lacked.

29. FROM William of Poitiers, 216. Translation, *English Historical Documents*, ii. 230.

[The Norman campaign of 1066 after Hastings].
The duke thereupon continued his advance on all fronts as it pleased him, and, crossing the river Thames both by ford and bridge at the same time, came to the borough [*oppidum*] of Wallingford. There Stigand the metropolitan bishop [*i.e.* of Canterbury] came in to him, did homage to him[27] and swore fealty,[28] renouncing the Æthling whom he had recklessly elected [*i.e.* as king].

30. FROM William of Poitiers, 238.

[1067. Concerning the Norman settlement of England].
In the castles [*castellis*] he placed capable custodians, brought over from France, in whose loyalty no less than ability he trusted, together with large numbers of horse and foot. He distributed rich fiefs [*opulenta beneficia*] amongst them, in return for which they would willingly undertake hardships and dangers. But to no Frenchmen was there given anything unjustly taken from an Englishman.

31. FROM Ordericus Vitalis, *The Ecclesiastical History* [Book iv, *c.*1125], ed. M. Chibnall with translation (Oxford, 1969), ii. 218.

[Concerning events and rebellion in Norman England and the king's first northern expedition, 1068].
To meet the danger the king rode to all the remote parts of the kingdom and fortified suitable places against enemy attacks. For the fortresses [*munitiones*] which the Gauls call 'castles' [*castella*] had been very few in the English provinces, and for this reason the English, although warlike and courageous, had nevertheless shown themselves too weak to withstand their enemies. The king thus built a castle at Warwick and committed it to the keeping of Henry son of Roger de Beaumont. Then Edwin and Morcar with their men, weighing the uncertain issue of battle, and not unreasonably preferring peace to war, sought the king's pardon and obtained it at least to outward appearance. Whereupon the king built Nottingham castle and entrusted it to William Peverel.

When the men of York heard this they avoided hostilities by

---

[27] *manibus ei sese dedit, lit.* 'gave himself to him by/with the hands', i.e. did homage by the *immixtio manuum.*
[28] *fidem sacramento confirmavit.*

immediate and unconditional surrender, and gave the king both the keys of the city and hostages. The king, however, because he doubted their loyalty, fortified a castle[29] [*munitionem firmavit*] in the city and put it in the custody of chosen knights. [*Both the Northumbrian noble, Archill, and Malcolm king of Scots then made peace with the king, the latter through the mediation of bishop Æthelwine of Durham*]. After these events, the king, as he returned [*i.e.* south], sited castles at Lincoln, Huntingdon and Cambridge, and committed their keeping to the strongest barons.

32. FROM Ordericus Vitalis, 260–6.

[Concerning the Norman settlement, c.1071].

After king William had overthrown, as I have said, the great Mercian earls – Edwin being dead, and Morcar confined in prison – he distributed the chief regions of England amongst his followers, and raised up the richest tribunes and centurians from even the lowest of his Norman dependents. . . .[30]

[*There follows detailed information about the grants made by William to his principal companions – including William fitz Osbern, Walter de Lacy, Hugh of Avranches, Roger of Montgomery, Walter Giffard, William de Warenne, Hugh de Grandmesnil, Henry de Ferrers, Odo, bishop of Bayeux, and Goeffrey, bishop of Coutances – often with personal information, sometimes entertaining : thus of Hugh of Avranches, given the county of Chester, Orderic remarks*]: He was not so much generous as prodigal; he always led about with him not just a household but an army.[31] He kept no reckoning either of what he gave or what he received. His hunting was a daily devastation of his land, for he thought more highly of fowlers and huntsmen than he did of the cultivators of the soil or the spokesmen of heaven. He was the slave of gluttony; weighed down by a mountain of fat he could hardly move. He was devoted to carnal lusts. From his concubines he begat a numerous progeny of both sexes. . . . Likewise Eustace count of Boulogne, Robert of Mortain,[32] William of Evreux, and Robert of Eu and Geoffrey son of Rotrou of Mortagne, together with other earls and magnates too numerous to name, received from king William great revenues and honors [*honores*] in England. So foreigners were enriched with the wealth of England, while her own sons were driven out to be exiles without hope in foreign realms. It is said that the king himself received each day from the ordinary revenues

---

[29] Site of the present Clifford's Tower.
[30] 'made the humblest of the Normans men of wealth with civil and military authority' (Chibnall).
[31] *non familiam secum sed exercitum semper ducebat.*
[32] With Odo of Bayeux a half-brother of the Conqueror.

of England £1061 10s 1½d sterling, without counting royal taxes, the profits of justice [*reatum redemptionibus*] and innumerable other receipts which daily swelled the royal coffers. King William carefully surveyed his whole kingdom, and had a careful description made of all its fiscal resources [*fiscos*] as they were in the time of king Edward.[33] He also allocated lands to knights [*militibus*] in such a way and so arranged their contingents [*ordines*] that the kingdom of England should always have 60,000 knights [*milites*] at the ready, and produce them immediately on the king's command as necessity required.

33. FROM William of Malmesbury, *Gesta Pontificum Anglorum* [*c*.1125], ed. N. E. S. A. Hamilton (Rolls Series, London, 1872), 253.

[Concerning the construction of the castle of Worcester, *c*.1066–9].
The sheriff of Worcester appointed by the king was Urse,[34] who constructed a castle [*castellum*] at the monks' very throat [*in ipsis pene faucibus monachorum*], in that the fosse cut off part of their cemetery. Complaint was made to the archbishop,[35] who was the guardian of the bishopric. He, when he had seen Urse, began with these words: 'Hattest thou Urs, have thou Godes kurs'. Thus felicitously spoken but playing harshly upon the euphony of names: 'Thou art called Urse', he said, 'and may you have the curse of God, and' – which I have not put in English – 'my curse and the curse of all the priesthood if you do not move that castle [*castellum*] from here. And you may know for sure that your progeny will not long inherit from the land of St. Mary.' Thus he spoke that those things might be fulfilled which we now see fulfilled. Not many years afterwards his [Urse's] son Roger was driven from the paternal inheritance which he then possessed, by the serious displeasure of king Henry [I], because in hasty rage he had ordered one of the king's officials to be killed.

34. FROM William of Malmesbury, *Gesta Pontificum*, 281.

[Concerning Wulfstan bishop of Worcester].
As I have already said, he was abstemious in food and drink, although in his hall, in the manner of the English, there was drinking to all hours after dinner. When he sat at table with them he ruminated on the psalms, though pretending to drink in his turn. While others drained great foaming tankards, he, holding the smallest goblet in his hand, encouraged them to make merry, though honouring thus the custom of the country rather than the judgement of his heart. Nor did he disregard

---

[33] I.e. the Domesday Survey of 1086.
[34] Urse d'Abitot.
[35] Ealdred of York.

the customs of the Normans, but was accompanied by a retinue of knights [*pompam militum secum ducens*] who were an absolute ruination in their annual stipends and daily food.

35. FROM *The Vita Wulfstani of William of Malmesbury* [*c.*1124–1143, but based upon an earlier life of Wulfstan bishop of Worcester by Coleman, monk of Worcester, *c.*1095–1113], ed. R. R. Darlington (Camden Third Series, xl, London, 1928), 46–7.

Except when he took his meals with the monks, he always dined publicly in hall with the knights [*militibus*]. For it would have been thought improper and ill-mannered if he had eaten in private, while the rest of the household grumbled.

36. FROM the *Chronicon Monasterii de Abingdon* [relevant part mid-12th century], ed. J. Stevenson (Rolls Series, London, 1858), ii. 3. Translation, *English Historical Documents*, ii. 902.

Concerning the knights [*milites*] of this our church. In the early days of his coming to the abbey [abbot Athelhelm][36] went nowhere unless surrounded by a force of armed knights [*armatorum . . . militum*]. And indeed it was necessary to do this. For the many rumours of conspiracies against the king and his realm coming in daily from all parts compelled everyone in England to protect himself. Then castles [*castella*] were raised at Wallingford, Oxford, and Windsor, and at many other places, for the defence of the kingdom. Hence this abbey was ordered by royal command to have a guard of knights [*militum excubias*] at that same Windsor castle [*oppidum*].[37] Wherefore in such circumstances knights [*milites*] from overseas coming into England were regarded with special favour.

The affairs of the kingdom being in such a state of uproar, the lord abbot Athelhelm safely guarded with a strong force of knights [*militum*] the place committed to him [i.e. Windsor castle]; and at first indeed he used stipendiaries [*stipendiarios*] for this purpose. But after the disturbances had died down, since it was noted in the annals [*in Annalibus*][38] by command of the king how many knights [*milites*] were to be exacted from bishops and abbots for the defence of the realm when need should

[36] He was appointed from Jumièges to take the place of the deposed and imprisoned abbot Ealdred *c.* 1071.
[37] A writ of Henry I commanding the barons of the abbey to do their castle-guard at Windsor as they did in the time of Rufus will be found in the same Abingdon Chronicle (ii. 90. Cf. *Regesta Regum Anglo-Normannorum*, ii, ed. C. Johnson and H. A. Cronne, Oxford, 1956, No. 725).
[38] Yearly records, year-rolls?

arise, the abbot, having previously refrained from such grants, thenceforth assigned to kinsmen [*pertinentibus*] manors from the church's possessions, in each case in return for stipulated service from the manor thus given.[39] These lands had been held by those called thegns [*Tahinos*], who had fallen in the battle of Hastings.

37. FROM the *Liber Eliensis* [mid-12th century], ed. E. O. Blake (Camden Third Series xcii, London, 1962), 216–18.

Ch. 134. At this time [1072] the whole of Scotland with her hordes of warriors sought to rebel against our king William and overthrow him. He, nothing daunted, went against them with a combined force of horse and ships. . . . For he had commanded both the abbots and bishops of all England to send their due knight service [*debita militie obsequia*] and he established that from that time forward contingents of knights [*militum . . . presidia*] should be provided by them to the kings of England in perpetual right for their military expeditions, and that no one, however highly placed, should presume to oppose this edict, and thus he trampled underfoot the just and ancient liberties of the English church, never ceasing to harass it beyond endurance as though he would extinguish it entirely. And when these things were known to the abbot of Ely, he bitterly bewailed the endless troubles of his house, and sadly took counsel with the brethren as to what he should do, so that in such a crisis they, like good sons, might comfort him, and protect the peace of that place by devout prayer to the mercy of their holy mother Etheldreda, and not refrain from openly declaring what they thought the best course of action. From them he received the advice to go at once to the king's majesty . . . [*i.e. to plead the liberty of St. Etheldreda, not to be violated* 'by new and intolerable exactions'] . . . But the king spurned his [the abbot's] prayers and gifts alike, would not revoke the evil regulation,[40] but intending rather to increase the burden, commanded him at the royal will [*ex nutu regis*] to keep a garrison of 40 knights [*custodiam xl militum*] in the isle [*i.e. of Ely*]. Whereupon the abbot sorrowfully withdrew, collected knights [*milites*] – who were, however, well-born dependents and adherents of his[41] – bestowed arms on many of them, and maintained according to custom the number predetermined by the king's command within the hall of the church [*habuitque ex consuetudine secundum iussum regis pretaxatum militie numerum infra aulam ecclesie*], receiving their daily provisions and wages from the hand of the

---

[39] *edicto cuique tenore parendi de suae portionis mansione.*
[40] *malo statuta convelli non desinit.*
[41] *clientes autem et ingenuos, qui sibi adherebant*: presumably the sense is that (as opposed to the complaint at many other houses) there was no question here of nepotism or influence. Cf. below.

cellarer, an arrangement which could and did cause intolerable and unendurable disturbances. In consequence therefore the abbot, under compulsion and not as a matter of the influence and favour of the rich or of devotion to his own relatives, allowed the intruders [*invasoribus*]⁴² upon certain of the lands of St. Etheldreda to hold them in fee [*in feudum*]⁴³ – as for example Picot the sheriff, Hardwin de Scalers, Roger Bigod, Hervey de Bourges and others, as the book of lands⁴⁴ sets forth – but alienating scarcely any demesne land, so that they would serve the king in all military expeditions and the church be henceforth untroubled. . . . Ch. 135. William, surnamed Rufus, therefore succeeded his father in the kingdom [1087], but soon a serious discord about the succession arose among the magnates of the realm, some, the minority, supporting the king, the others supporting his brother Robert, on the advice especially of bishops Geoffrey of Coutances, William of Durham and Odo of Bayeux, who wanted either to hand him over alive to his brother Robert or take the kingdom from him dead. The king therefore, seeing himself threatened by so great a danger, now violently exacted from the churches the due service [*debitum servitium*] which his father had imposed, and the English church was beset on every side with innumerable troubles. He compelled eighty knights of the abbey of Ely to be provided as due to him in the campaign, without any reduction, forty of whom, that is to say, being those whom his father had ordered to be kept as a garrison in the isle. And when abbot Samson learnt of this he groaned in spirit, calling upon God to be the judge of those things which were done to him.

38. FROM Matthew Paris, *Historia Anglorum* [thirteenth century, based upon Roger of Wendover], ed. F. Madden (Rolls Series, London, 1866–9), i. 13 [cf. Roger of Wendover, *Flores Historiarum*, ed. H. O. Coxe, London, 1841–4, ii. 7].

In the year of Our Lord 1070 king William . . . also placed all the bishoprics and abbeys, who hitherto had been free from all secular service, under military service [*sub servitute . . . militari*], enrolling [the said] bishoprics and abbeys according to his will [*inrotulans episcopatus et abbatias pro voluntate sua*], how many knights he wished to be provided from each to him and his successors in time of war.

39. FROM Galbert of Bruges, *Histoire du meurtre de Charles le Bon*,

⁴² I.e. those who had (according to the abbey) unjustly 'invaded' and seized Ely lands in the course of the Norman conquest and settlement – a process from which Ely suffered especially as the result of her involvement in Hereward's revolt. See Miller, *Abbey and Bishopric of Ely*, 66–8.
⁴³ Thus providing the needed knight-service.
⁴⁴ Probably the surviving survey, *Inquisitio Eliensis*.

comte de Flandre, ed. H. Pirenne (Paris, 1892), 89. Also ed., translation only, J. B. Ross, *The Murder of Charles the Good, Count of Flanders by Galbert of Bruges* (New York, 1967), 206–7. Quoted and translated, Ganshof, *Feudalism*, 65, 111.

[April, 1127, Count William Clito receives the vassals of his predecessor].
First they did homage [*hominium*] in this way. The count asked each one if he wished without reserve to become his man [*homo suus*], and he replied 'I wish it', and with hands clasped and enclosed by the hands of the count, they were bound together by a kiss. Secondly, he who had done homage pledged his faith [to the count] in these words: 'I promise by my faith that from this time forward I will be faithful to count William and will maintain my homage to him entirely against every person, in good faith and without deception'. Thirdly he swore this on the relics of saints. Then, with a wand which he held in his hand, the count gave investiture [*investituram*] to all those who in this compact had promised fealty and done homage and taken an oath.

40. FROM *The Alexiad of Anna Comnena*, ed. (translation only) E. R. A. Sewter (Harmondsworth, 1969) [the twelfth-century biography of the Byzantine Emperor Alexius I Comnenus by Anna, his daughter], 415–16.

They [the Byzantine army] were issued with a plentiful supply of arrows and told not to be at all niggardly in their use; but they were to shoot at the horses rather than the [Franks], for he [Alexius] knew that cuirasses and coats of mail made them almost if not entirely invulnerable . . . [Frankish] armour consists of a tunic interwoven with iron rings linked one with another; the iron is of good quality, capable of resisting an arrow and giving protection to the soldier's body. This armour is supplemented by a shield, not round but long, broad at the top and tapering to a point; inside it is slightly curved; the outside is smooth and shiny, and it has a flashing, bronze boss. . . . There was another reason for shooting at the horses: the [Franks] when they dismounted would be easily handled. A mounted [Frank] is irresistible; he would bore his way through the walls of Babylon.

41. FROM Bertran de Born[?], late 12th-century. Ed. C. Appel, *Bertran von Born*, (Halle, 1931), No. 40. Quoted and translated, Marc Bloch, *Feudal Society*, translated by L. A. Manyon (London, 1961), 293.

I love the gay Eastertide, which brings forth leaves and flowers; and I

I *

love the joyous songs of the birds, re-echoing through the copse. But also I love to see, amidst the meadows, tents and pavilions spread; and it gives me great joy to see, drawn up in the field, knights and horses in battle array; and it delights me when the scouts scatter people and herds in their path; and I love to see them followed by a great body of men-at-arms; and my heart is filled with gladness when I see strong castles besieged, and the stockades broken and overwhelmed, and the warriors on the bank, girt about by fosses, with a line of strong stakes interlaced. . . . Maces, swords, helms of different hues, shields that will be riven and shattered as soon as the fight begins; and many vassals struck down together; and the horses of the dead and the wounded roving at random. And when battle is joined, let all men of good lineage think of naught but the breaking of heads and arms; for it is better to die than to be vanquished and live. I tell you, I find no such savour in food, or in wine, or in sleep, as in hearing the shout 'On! On!' from both sides, and the neighing of steeds that have lost their riders, and the cries of 'Help! Help!'; in seeing men great and small go down on the grass beyond the fosses; in seeing at last the dead, with the pennoned stumps of lances still in their sides.

B. Charters, Leases, Writs and Similar Documents

42. The 'Memorandum' of Oswald bishop of Worcester to king Edgar concerning the leases he has been granting [c.963–75], from Hemming's cartulary [late 11th century], ed. T. Hearne, *Hemingi Chartularium Ecclesiae Wigornensis* (Oxford, 1723), i. 292–6.

Heading [in Heming][1] *Indiculum* of the liberty of Oswaldslow Hundred. I, Oswald, bishop of the church of Worcester, give thanks before God and man to my most beloved lord, Edgar, king of the English, for all the gifts bestowed upon me by his clemency. So, if God's grace will allow, before God and man I will be for ever faithful to him, remembering, with gratitude, his unfailing liberality, because he has granted to me that which I especially desired, through intermediaries, namely the most reverend archbishop Dunstan, and the venerable Æthelwold, bishop of Winchester, and the noble ealdorman Brihtnoth, through whose good offices he has received my complaint and that of the holy church of God, and has granted just redress by the counsel of his wise men and magnates, to the benefit of the church which he has generously and graciously committed to my rule. Wherefore it pleased both me and those my patrons and counsellors that, with the permission and attestation of my lord the said king, I should set out clearly in detail in the form of a chirograph for my brothers, the bishops who will succeed me, in what manner I have been granting to the faithful men subject to me the lands which have been committed to my charge, for the term of three lives, that is, of the grantee and two heirs after him, so that they [my successors] may know what they ought justly to take from them, according to the agreement made with them and according to their engagement, wherefore also I have taken pains to draw up this letter as a precaution, lest anyone, instigated by malignant greed, wishing to alter this in future time, should seek to abjure the service of the church. Therefore this agreement was made with them, my said lord the king assenting, and by his attestation corroborating and confirming the abundance of his munificence, and with all the wise men and magnates of his realm attesting and consenting. I have granted the lands of holy church to them to hold under me on these terms, namely that they shall fulfil the whole law of riding as riding men should [*ut omnis equitandi lex ab eis impleatur, que ad equites pertinet*],[2] and that they shall pay in full

[1] It is to be noted that the memorandum itself makes no specific reference to Oswaldslow.

[2] The familiar translation is that of Maitland, *Domesday Book and Beyond*, 359.

all those things which justly belong to the right of the said church, that is to say those which in English are called church-scot, and toll, and *tacc* or *swinesceade*,[3] and the other dues of the church, unless the bishop shall have pardoned anything to anyone, and they shall swear that so long as they hold the said lands they will continue humbly subject to the commands of the bishop with all submission. In addition, they shall hold themselves available to supply all the needs of the bishop, they shall lend horses, they shall ride themselves, and, moreover, be ready to build bridges and do all that is necessary in burning lime for the work of the church.[4] They shall be prepared to make deer-hedges for the bishop's hunting, and they must send their own hunting spears to the chase whenever the lord bishop wishes. Further, to meet the many other wants of the bishop, whether to fulfil the service due to him or that due to the king, they shall always with all humility and submissiveness be subject to the authority and will of that *archiductor*[5] who presides over the bishopric, on account of the benefice [*beneficium*] which is leased [*prestitum*] to them, according to his command and the amount of land which each possesses. When, however, the aforesaid term has run out, that is to say the term of the lives of two heirs after those presently in possession, it shall be entirely at the bishop's discretion, whatever decision he reaches being final, whether he retains those lands to his own use, if he judges it best, or whether he leases them to someone else for a further term, if it pleases him, so that, as need requires, the services of the church, as described above, may always be fully rendered. And if there shall be any malicious withholding of any of the aforesaid dues, the default shall be made good in accordance with the right of the bishop, or gift and land shall be confiscated from him who possessed them. And if, which passes belief, there should be any man who, at the instigation of the devil, should be tempted through our grant [*beneficium*] to deprive the church of God by fraud or force of her possession and due service, he shall be deprived of our blessing, and the blessing of God and his saints, unless he make the fullest amends and restore all things as they were before. For it is written that the plunderers and despoilers of God's kingdom shall not succeed. Now therefore, in the name of God, and of St. Mary in whose name this monastery is dedicated, I declare and command that no one shall dare in any way to transgress this which, as laid down and described above, shall last for ever. Whosoever shall keep it shall be replete with blessing, and whosoever goes against it shall be cursed by God and all the saints. Amen.

[3] Payment for swine-pasture.

[4] Maitland, 359–60 and n., suggested this rendering of the obscure *ad totum piramiticum opus ecclesiae calcis*, taking *piramiticus* (from the Greek) to mean 'of or belonging to fire'.

[5] A literal translation would be 'chief leader' or 'commander in chief'.

[*The bishop calls down God's grace upon the king, and ends*]:
There are three copies of these letters as title and claim: one in that same city which is called Worcester; another with the venerable archbishop Dunstan in Canterbury; the third with bishop Æthelwold in the city of Winchester.

43. Lease of Oswald, archbishop of York and bishop of Worcester, to Goding [not later than 985]. Printed with translation, A. J. Robertson, *Anglo-Saxon Charters*, (Cambridge, 1939), No. lxi; also in Hemming's cartulary, ed. Hearne, i. 139-41.

Bredicot and *Genenofer*, to Goding.

I, Oswald, archbishop by the grace of God, with the consent and leave of Æthelred, King of England, and Earl Ælfric and the community at Worcester, have freely granted a certain piece of land, namely 3 hides at Bredicot [Worcs.] and a yardland at the place called *Genenofer*, to a certain cleric whose name is Goding, with everything pertaining thereto for his lifetime, and after his death to two heirs of his own choice, and after their death to the holy foundation at Worcester for the use of the bishop. And I grant him in addition 7 acres of meadow in the river pasture belonging to Tibberton – 3½ acres in one place and 3½ acres in another, as it may fittingly be divided. We convey to him likewise the messuage which he has before the gate, and to two heirs after his death.

These are the boundaries of the 3 hides at Bredicot, namely first from the bare hill in front of the old dyke, along the old dyke to the famous (?) site, from the famous (?) site back to the dyke, along the dyke as far as the saltway, then west over the saltway to the hedged enclosure at the Spetchley boundary, from the Spetchley boundary along the slope to the west of the oxen's pasture, from the oxen's pasture north to the hedged enclosure, along the hedged enclosure to the dirty bog, from the dirty bog to the dyke, from the dyke to the white (?) meadow by the made way, along the made way to the little hill, then from the hill past the four thornbushes, from the thornbushes along the headlands to the thorny headland, from the headland to the hedged enclosure, along the hedged enclosure to the Honey Bourne, along the Honey Bourne to the dyke, from the dyke to the little bog, from the bog to the old dyke, along the dyke to the foreside of the heath, then south along the little dyke, then westward over the heath to the little grove, from the grove southward to the east of the wolfpit, thereafter along the path back to the bare hill in front of the dyke.

This estate, moreover, shall be free from every duty of a secular nature except the repair of bridges and fortifications and military service against enemies. May St. Mary and St. Michael, with St. Peter and all the saints of God, have mercy on those who uphold this. If anyone, without due cause, attempts to break it, he shall have to account for it to God on the last day of his life, unless he has set about making amends.

Here are the signatures . . . [*The names of seventeen witnesses with their crosses, follow, beginning with those of archbishop Oswald*].

44. Lease of Ealdred bishop of Worcester to Wulfgeat [1046–1053: probably 1051–2]. Printed with translation, Robertson, *Anglo-Saxon Charters*, No. cxi.

Here it is declared in this document that Bishop Ealdred has granted to Wulfgeat a certain piece of land, namely 1½ hides in the manor called Ditchford [Worcs.], to be held and enjoyed for three lives, and after their time the estate shall return once more to the disposal of him who is in control of the bishopric of Worcester at the time. And they shall always be submissive and obedient and acknowledge the lordship of whoever is bishop at the time, and if they are guilty of any defection, they shall forfeit the property.

The witnesses of this are all the community at Worcester and the community at Evesham and the community at Pershore and Earl Leofric and Earl Odda and Ælfric his brother and Brihtric, Ælfgar's son, and Owine and Wagen and Æthelric, the bishop's brother, and Ceolmaer and Atser and Esbearn and Ordwig and Æthelstan the Fat and Ælfweard of Longdon and all the leading thegns in Worcestershire, both Danish and English.

And at the king's summons the holder shall discharge the obligations on these 1½ hides at the rate of one, for three lives.

45. Narrative concerning Crowle, Worcs., from Hemming's cartulary, ed. Hearne, i. 264–5. The events related evidently took place in the first half of the eleventh century. Leofric, established as earl of Mercia by Cnut, died in 1057. Simund still held Crowle in 1066 (*Domesday Book*, i. 174). This Crowle is Crowle Siward in 1336 when the monks finally recovered it (*Cartulary of Worcester Cathedral Priory*, ed. R. R. Darlington, Pipe Roll Society, New Series lxxvi, London, 1968, 284).

[*Heading*] Concerning Crowle: At that time when the Danes were in possession of this country, the manor [*villa*] called Crowle was lost from the demesne of the monks [*a dominico victu monachorum*] in this way, although the service of the church has so far, by God's grace, been kept. For a certain Simund, a Dane and a housecarl [*miles*] of Leofric, earl of the Mercians, being in possession of the other and neighbouring

Crowle, coveted, as was habitual with the men of that race, what was then our own manor also. Which, when he could by no means obtain it, by his own power and influence and that of his lord he did it so much damage by injuries and pleas that he almost made in uninhabited. Hence, after [yet another] lawsuit, at the request of Simund's lord, the aforesaid earl, Æthelwine thc prior of this monastery granted him the same land to possess during his lifetime, on this condition however, that he should serve the monastery for it on military expeditions by land and sea (which were then frequent),[6] and acknowledge the prior's lordship by the annual render of money or a horse.

46. FROM the memorandum or record of a great plea held at Worcester in the Conqueror's reign, by authority of the king's writ sent from Normandy and in the presence of Geoffrey, bishop of Coutances, on the king's behalf, between Wulfstan bishop of Worcester and Walter abbot of Evesham, in which the former is successful, concerning lands in Bengeworth (Worcs.) and Hampton (Worcs.), which the bishop claims are held of him by the abbot for all due service. From Hemming's cartulary, ed. Hearne, i. 80–3.

This is the record of the plea between W[ulfstan] the bishop and Walter abbot of Evesham, that is, that the said bishop claimed against the said abbot sake and soke and burial-fees [sepulturam] and church-scot and suit of court [requisitiones] and all customs pertaining to the church of Worcester in the hundred of Oswaldslow, and the king's geld, and service [servitium], and military expeditions by land and sea [expeditiones in terra et in mari], in respect of fifteen hides in Hampton and four hides in Bengeworth, which the abbot ought to hold of the bishop, as the other enfeoffed men [feudati] of the church freely hold in return for the service due to both king and bishop.[7]

[The abbot denies this but can only bring relics upon which to swear in support of his contention; whereas the bishop brings in witnesses ready to confirm his claim on oath]: Of whom one was Edric, who in the time of king Edward [i.e. the Confessor] was the steersman [stermannus] of the bishop's ship and the leader of the forces of the same bishop to the king's service.[8]

47. Writ of William I to Æthelwig abbot of Evesham [1072? before 1077]. Printed, Round, Feudal England, 304; Stubbs, Select Charters, 97. Translation, English Historical Documents, ii. 895.

---

[6] ut pro ea ipse ad expeditionem terra marique (que tunc crebro agebatur) monasterio serviret.
[7] sicut alii feudati ecclesie ad omne debitum servitium regis et episcopi libere tenent.
[8] ductor exercitus ejusdem episcopi ad servitium regis.

W. king of the English to Æthelwig abbot of Evesham greeting. I command you to summon all those who are under your administration and jurisdiction so that they have all the knights [milites] which they owe me fully equipped before me at Clarendon on the octaves of Whitsun. You also on that day are to come to me and bring with you, fully equipped, those five knights [milites] which you owe me from your abbey. Witnessed by Eudo the dapifer. At Winchester.

48. Charter of Baldwin abbot of Bury St. Edmunds in favour of Peter, a knight of king William [1066–1087 and probably early in the reign]. Printed by D. C. Douglas, Feudal Documents from the Abbey of Bury St. Edmunds (London, 1962), No. 168. Translation, English Historical Documents, ii. 896–7.[9]

Be it known to you all that Peter a knight [miles] of king William will be the feudal man [feodalis homo i.e. vassal] of St. Edmunds and abbot Baldwin by homage [manibus junctis][10] with the king's permission and the consent of the monks, with that service only which is set down in this document, saving the king's fealty [fidelitas], having received the fee [feodum] freely, less six royal forfeitures. Peter promises that he will serve the abbot within the kingdom[11] . . . with three or four knights [militibus] and at his own expense. If as the abbot's attorney he pleads anywhere within the kingdom, this shall be at his own expense.[12] But if the abbot shall take him with him everywhere[13] this shall be at the abbot's expense. In addition he shall make available a knight [militem] within or without the kingdom wherever and whenever the abbot wishes to have one with him in his retinue.[14] This is the description of the fee. [The description which follows is in terms of tenants and tenements: e.g. 'The land of Edric the blind with 24 freemen and as many villeins']. Witnesses on the abbot's part: Robert Flauus, Frodo, Robert de Vaus, Arnulf, Fulcher, Burgard, Goscelin. On Peter's part: Randulf, Richard,

---

[9] The charter survives only in fourteenth-century copies with evident corruptions. Any such corrupt passage I have omitted as being both untranslatable and likely to confuse, though giving the Latin of the omission in a footnote.

[10] i.e. the immixtio manuum.

[11] In Douglas' text the following passage, here omitted, reads: 'si priusquam ex parte regis ex abbatis parte monetur in antecedentibus uel subsequentibus expedicionis regie custodiis'. The sense may be that in this respect Peter will serve the abbot as he formerly served the king: in any event this whole sentence is dealing with military knight-service as opposed to the knightly and vassalic escort and legal duties of the following sentences.

[12] The variant reading sustentabitur seems preferable here to the sustentabuntur of Douglas' edition.

[13] i.e. presumably about the country in his itinerant household.

[14] ut suum proprium militem habere voluerit.

Hardwyn, Philip, Ralph Facheiz, William son of Robert, Turold the butterfly (papilio). And many others on both parts who all confirm that the abbot did not give to Peter either soke or sake over his freemen, and this is true.

49. Charter of abbot Gilbert [Crispin] and the convent of Westminster to William Baynard (1083). Printed, J. Armitage Robinson, *Gilbert Crispin*, 38. Translation, *English Historical Documents*, ii. 895–6.

In the year of the Incarnation of Our Lord 1083.[15] We abbot Gilbert and the convent of Westminster have granted to William Baynard a certain berewick[16] of the vill [*villa*] of Westminster, called Totenhala, for his lodging and to hold for the whole of his life, for the service of one knight [*pro servicio unius militis*], with all things pertaining thereto, as well and as freely [*bene et quiete*] as ever Wulfric the thegn [*taynus*], surnamed Bordewayte, ever held it from the church. And the said William shall have the customs and liberties which we have in it, except our aids [*auxilia*] which we shall take there as from our knights [*militibus nostris*] in the other lands of the church, and except for the tithes of that land attached to the house of our almonry.[17] These things we grant him to hold for the love and service which he has borne towards our church, but on this condition that after his death that land shall remain to our church freely and without disturbance. And in addition the aforesaid William has pledged his faith to us that he will not sell the said land, nor put it in gage, nor alienate it to anyone to the loss of our church. Witnessed by Robert the prior, Nicholas, William and Herbert, monks, Ralph Baynard, Herluin the brother of Grunzo, and many others.

50. Charter of Robert [Losinga] bishop of Hereford to Roger son of Walter [de Lacy], 1085. Printed with facsimile, V. H. Galbraith, 'An episcopal landgrant of 1085,' *English Historical Review*, xliv, (1929). Translation, *English Historical Documents*, ii. 897.

This privilege [*priuilegium*] between himself and Roger son of Walter Robert bishop of the church of Hereford commanded to be set down concerning certain land called Hamme [now Holme Lacy] and those things which pertain to it, which land belongs to the church of St. Mary the Mother of God and of St. Ethelbert the Martyr, and the aforesaid

---

[15] The charter survives only in a later copy and the date may be an incorrec·
addition. It is, however, without doubt a very early charter of enfeoffment of *c.*
1083.
[16] An outlying member of a manor.
[17] *exceptis decimis . . . domui elemosinarie nostre constitutis.*

bishop held it in his own demesne [*in proprio dominio*] for the support of the church and of himself. This land the aforesaid knight [*miles*], that is to say, Roger, requested from the bishop by the influence of friends and by the offer of money.[18] But the bishop by the counsel of his men granted him the said land by this agreement, that he would serve him [the bishop] with two knights [*militibus*] as his father did whenever it should be necessary; and by the further agreement that the bishop's men of Hamtuna [Hampton] and of Hereford and those who belong to that land [*i.e.* Holme Lacy] may take timber from the wood, but only for the use of the bishop, as much as he shall require for fuel and for the repair of [his] manors; and the bishop's pigs, but his only, from the same manors may be grazed in the said wood. And furthermore, if Roger should become a monk, or die, neither his mother, nor his wife, nor his sons, nor his brothers, nor any relative of his shall enter that land, but the bishop whoever he shall then be shall recover it to the benefit of holy church and of himself without any contradiction whatsoever. This was done in the year of the Incarnation of Our Lord 1085 in the eighth Indiction. These are the witnesses of this matter: earl Roger,[19] and Hugh his son, and Everard his other son, and the countess, and Warin the sheriff, Osbert son of Richard, Drogo fitz Pons, Gerard de Tornai, William Malbedan, Gilbert the constable of earl Roger. From the bishop's men: Gerard his brother, Hamfrid the archdeacon, Ansfrid the priest, William, Lewin, Alfward, Saulf, Alwin; together with the following laymen, Udo, Athalard, Franco, Arnulf, Tetbald, Robert, Gozo, Osbert, Peter, Richard the butler. From Roger's men: clerks, Raulf, Gosfrid, Odo, Gerold; laymen, Walter, Herbert de Furcis, Richard de Stantuna, Herman de Drewis, Robert de Baschevilla, Richard de Eschetot, William de Ebroia, Raulf de Salcet, Nicholas, Gotmund.

The aforesaid Roger also holds other land of the demesne [*de victu proprio*] of the bishop, namely Onibury by this agreement: as long as he lives he shall pay 20s. each year on the feast of St. Martin, and after his death, or equally if he shall become a monk, the land shall return to the bishop, in whatever condition it may then be,[20] without any contradiction. These are the witnesses of this matter: Ansfrid de Cormelis, Edric de Wendloc, the other Edric the dapifer, and all the above-said except earl Roger and his household.

51. Writ of William Rufus exacting relief from the free-tenants of the vacant bishopric of Worcester [1095, following the death of bishop Wulfstan]. From Hemming's Cartulary, ed. Hearne, i,

---

[18] *per amicos et per pecuniam.*
[19] Roger of Montgomery, earl of Shrewsbury.
[20] i.e. presumably, in whatever state or stage of husbandry it may then be in, e.g. with or without standing crops, improvement, development, etc.

79–80. Printed, Round, *Feudal England*, 309; Stubbs, *Select Charters*, 109 (extract only).

W[illiam] king of the English to all the French and English who hold free lands of the bishopric of Worcester, greeting. Know that, the bishop having died, the honor has come back into my hand. Now I will that from your lands you shall give me such relief as I have assessed by my barons. Hugh de Laci, £20. Walter Punher, £20. Gilbert son of Turold, £5. Robert the bishop,[21] £10. The abbot of Evesham, £30. Walter of Gloucester, £20. Roger son of Durand, £10.[22] Winebald de Balaon, £10. Drogo fitz Pons,[23] £10. Robert son of Sckilin, £5. Robert the steersman [*stirmannus*], £3.[24] Anschitil de Colesburna, £10. Roger de Cumtune, £1. Eudo, £3. William de Begebiri, £2. Richard and Franca, £5. Angot, £1. Berald, £1. William de Wic, £1. Robert son of Nigel, £5. Alric the archdeacon, £5. Orderic the dapifer, £40. Orderic Black [*blaca*, alias Niger], £5. Coleman, £2. Warin, 30s. Baldwin, £2. Swegen son of Azor, £1. Alfred, 30s. Siward, £2. Sawulf, £15. Algar, £2. Chipping, £1. Witnessed by Ranulf the chaplain,[25] and Eudo the dapifer, and Urse de Abetot. And if anyone refuses to do this, Urse and Bernard shall seize [his] lands and money into my hand.

52. FROM the Coronation Charter or Charter of Liberties of Henry I, 1100. Printed, Stubbs, *Select Charters*, 117–19; with translation, A. J. Robertson, *The Laws of the Kings of England from Edmund to Henry I* (Cambridge, 1925), 276–83.

Henry king of the English to Samson the bishop and Urse d'Abetot and all his barons and faithful men both French and English in Worcestershire, greeting . . .[26]

[1] Know that by God's mercy and the common counsel of the barons of the whole kingdom of England I have been crowned king of that same kingdom. And because the kingdom has been oppressed by unjust exactions, I, out of respect for God and the love which I bear towards you all, in the first place make free the holy church of God. . . . And I abolish all evil customs whereby the realm of England has been unjustly burdened, the which evil customs I here set down:

[2] If one of my barons, earls or tenants shall die, his heir shall not buy

[21] i.e. of Hereford.
[22] Written above this entry is the note, 'quit by the king's writ'.
[23] *filius Pontii.*
[24] Round by an oversight in transcription omitted the next three names, continuing with *Willelmus de Begebiri*. They are, however, included in his analysis of writ, *Feudal England*, 312.
[25] i.e. Ranulf Flambard.
[26] i.e. this surviving copy is of that sent to Worcestershire.

back his land as was done in the time of my brother but shall pay a just and lawful relief [*relevatio*] for it. And similarly the men of my barons shall pay a just and lawful relief for their lands to their lords.

[3] And if one of my barons or other men shall wish to give in marriage his daughter or sister or neice or [other] female relative, he shall discuss it with me; but I will neither take anything from him for this permission nor forbid him to bestow her, unless he wishes to marry her to my enemy. And if a baron or other man of mine, being deceased, leaves a daughter as heir, I will give her [in marriage] together with her land by the counsel of my barons. And if after the death of her husband a wife survives and has no children, she shall have her dower and marriage portion, and I will not give her in marriage except with her consent.

[4] If however a wife survives with children, she too shall have her dower and marriage portion, so long as she keeps herself chaste, and I will not give her [in marriage] except with her consent. And the guardian of the land and children shall be either the wife or some other close relative who has a better right. And I command that my barons shall similarly act with moderation towards the sons and daughters and wives of their men. . . .

[11] To knights [*militibus*] who serve for their lands by the hauberk[27] I grant of my own proper gift that the lands which they hold in demesne[28] shall be quit of all gelds and all work [*et ab omni opere*], so that, released from so great a burden, they may thus fully equip themselves with horses and arms, that they may be fit and ready for my service and for the defence of my realm. . . .

Witnessed by Maurice bishop of London, William bishop elect of Winchester and Gerard bishop of Hereford and earl Henry and earl Simon and Walter Gifard and Robert de Muntforte and Roger Bigod and Eudo the dapifer and Robert fitz Hamo and Robert Malet. At Westminster when I was crowned.

53. FROM a writ of Henry I concerning the holding of the shire and hundred courts [*c.*1108–1111]. Printed, Stubbs, *Select Charters*, 122; with translation, Robertson, *Laws of the Kings of England*, 286, 287.

Henry king of the English to Samson the bishop and Urse d'Abetot and all his barons both French and English of Worcestershire greeting.

Know that I grant and command that in future my county courts and

---

[27] *qui per loricas terras suas deserviunt* – clearly an echo of the Norman *feudum loricae* or *fief de haubert*, more commonly the *feudum militis* or knight's fee in English terminology.

[28] *terrae dominicarum carrucarum suarum* – *lit.* lands of their demesne ploughs.

hundred courts shall sit in those places and at those times, as they sat in the time of king Edward and not otherwise. . . .

. . . And if henceforth a plea shall arise concerning the partition or seizure of lands, if it is between my demesne barons [*inter dominicos barones meos, i.e.* tenants-in-chief] it shall be heard in my court. And if it is between vavassors of another baron of my honor [*i.e.* the kingdom], the plea shall be heard in the court of their lord. . . .

. . . Witnessed by R. bishop of London, and Roger the bishop, and Ranulf the chancellor and R. count of Meulan: at Reading.

C. Laws, Customs and Cognate Sources

54. FROM the laws of Ine of Wessex [*c.*688–94]. Printed, with translation, F. L. Attenborough, *The Laws of the Earliest English Kings*, (New York, 1963), 48, 49. Translation only, *English Historical Documents*, i. 368.

*c.*40. A ceorl's homestead [*worthig*] shall be fenced both winter and summer. If they are not enclosed, and a beast belonging to his neighbour strays in through the opening he has left, he shall have no claim on that beast [but] he shall drive it out and suffer the damage.

55. FROM the laws of Ine of Wessex [*c.*688–94]. Printed, with translation, Attenborough, 50, 51; Stubbs, *Select Charters*, 68. Translation only, *English Historical Documents*, i. 369.

*c.*45. 120 shillings shall be paid for breaking into the residence [*burg*] of the king, or of the bishop within his diocese; 80 shillings for an ealdorman; 60 shillings for a king's thegn; 35 shillings for a nobleman holding land. The charge may be sworn off by oaths of corresponding value.

56. FROM the laws of Ine of Wessex [*c.*688–94]. Printed, with translation, Attenborough, 52, 53; Stubbs, *Select Charters*, 68. Translation only, *English Historical Documents*, i. 370.

*c.*51. If a nobleman [*gesithcund mon*] who holds land neglects the fyrd, he shall pay 120 shillings and forfeit his land; a nobleman who does not hold land shall pay 60 shillings; a ceorlish man shall pay 30 shillings, as the fine for neglect of military service [*fierdwite*].

57. FROM Alfred's laws [*c.*871–99]. Printed, with translation, Attenborough, 82, 83. Translation only, *English Historical Documents*, i. 379.

c.40. 120 shillings shall be paid for breaking into the king's residence [*burg*]; 90 shillings for an archbishop; 60 shillings for another bishop or ealdorman; 15 shillings for a man whose wergeld[1] is 1200 shillings; 15 shillings for one whose wergeld is 600 shillings; for breaking into a ceorl's enclosure [*edor*], 5 shillings.

[1] i.e. blood-price.

58. FROM the laws of Cnut, II, Secular Ordinance [c.1020–23]. Printed, with translation, A. J. Robertson, *Laws of the Kings of England from Edmund to Henry I*, 181; Stubbs, *Select Charters*, 86. Translation only, *English Historical Documents*, i. 420.

c.12. These are the rights that the king has over all men in Wessex; namely *mundbryce*[2] and *hamsocn*,[3] *forsteal*[4] and *fyrdwite* [i.e. the fine for neglect of military service], unless he will honour any man more highly. c.15. And in the Danelaw he has *fiht-wite*[5] and *fyrdwite*, *grithbryce*[6] and *hamsocne* unless he will honour any man more highly.

59. Of Oaths [c.920]. Printed, with translation, Stubbs, *Select Charters*, 73–4.

Thus shall a man swear fealty oaths [*hyldathas*]. By the Lord before whom this relic is holy, I will be to N. faithful and true, and love all that he loves, and shun all that he shuns, according to God's law, and according to secular custom; and never, willingly or intentionally, by word or by work, do aught of what is loathful to him; on condition that he keep me as I am willing to deserve, and all that fulfil that our agreement was, when I to him submitted and chose his will.

60. FROM 'Of People's Ranks and Laws' or a compilation on status. [c.1002–1023]. Printed with translation, Stubbs, *Select Charters*, 88–9; translation only, *English Historical Documents*, i, 432.

c.1. Once it used to be that people and rights went by dignities, and councillors of the people were then entitled to honour, each according to his rank, noble or peasant, retainer or lord. c.2. And if a ceorl prospered so that he possessed fully five hides of his own (church and kitchen),[7] a bell and a burgh-gate [*burh-geat*], a seat and special office in the king's hall, then was he thenceforth worthy of thegn-right. c.6. And if a merchant prospered, so that he thrice crossed the open sea at his own expense, then was he thenceforth worthy of thegn-right.

61. FROM the *Rectitudines Singularum Personarum* or *The Rights and Ranks of People* [first half of the eleventh century]. Printed

---

[2] Breach of the king's protection (*mund*).
[3] Attack on a homestead, including forcible entry and injury of those within.
[4] Obstruction, more particularly ambush.
[5] Fine for fighting.
[6] Breach of the king's peace (*grith*). Cf. *mundbryce* in c. 12 above.
[7] Words in parenthesis omitted in some texts.

F. Liebermann, *Die Gesetze der Angelsachsen* (Halle, 1903–16), i. 444–53. Translation, *English Historical Documents*, ii. 813.

Thegn's Law. The law of the thegn is, that he be entitled to his book-right[8] and that he shall contribute three things in respect of his land: armed service, and the repairing of fortresses and work upon bridges. Also in respect of many estates further services arise on the king's order, such as service connected with the deer fence at the king's residence, and equipping a guard ship, and guarding the coast, and guarding the lord, and military watch, alms-giving and church dues, and many other divers things.

62. FROM the '*Consuetudines et Justicie*' or 'The Customs and Rights of the duke of Normandy' [1091]. Printed, C. H. Haskins, *Norman Institutions*, New York, 1913 (reprinted New York and London, 1960), 281–4.

These are the customs and rights which the duke of Normandy has in his province, and which king William who acquired the kingdom of England strongly and strenuously maintained in his time, and which his sons Robert and William with the counsel of their bishops and barons at Caen recorded as written here. . . .

. . . [c.4]. No one in Normandy might dig a fosse in the open country [*in planam terram*] of more than one shovel's throw in depth,[9] nor set there more than one line of palisading, and that without battlements or alures.[10] And no one might make a fortification [*fortitudinem*] on the rock or in an island, and no one might raise a castle [*castellum*] in Normandy, and no one in Normandy might withhold the possession of his castle from the lord of Normandy[11] if he wished to take it into his own hand.

63. FROM the *Leges Henrici Primi* [early twelfth century], lv, i. Printed, Stubbs, *Select Charters*, 126. Translation only, *English Historical Documents*, ii. 461.

Every lord may summon his man in order to do justice upon him in his court; and if the man is resident in the most remote manor of that honor of which he holds, he shall nevertheless go to the plea if his lord shall summon him.

[8] i.e. land held by charter or 'land-book' with the privileges pertaining.

[9] *nisi tale quod de fundo potuisset terram iactare superius sine scabello.* The translation is difficult though the sense is clear.

[10] *sine . . . alatoriis*, i.e. the equivalent in timber of the wall-walk, a way or walk about the summit of the palisade facilitating its defence.

[11] *fortitudinem castelli sui vetare domino Normannie, lit.* deny the strength of his castle to the lord of Normandy?

64. FROM *The treatise on the laws and customs of the realm of England commonly called Glanville*, ed. G. D. H. Hall, (London, 1965), *lib*. IX, cc. i and viii (104, 112). For the latter, see also Stubbs, *Select Charters*, 193.

lib. IX, c. i. If anyone has done several homages for different fees to different lords who are attacking each other, and his liege lord commands him to go personally with him against another of his lords, he must obey his command in this matter, but saving to that other lord the service for the fee which he holds of him.

lib. IX, c. viii. There are in addition other occasions on which lords may take similar aids from their men in like manner ['*Glanville*' *has just discussed the taking of an aid by a lord for the payment of his own relief on succession, such an aid to be reasonable, not excessive, in amount*], as, for example, if the son and heir becomes a knight, or if the eldest daughter marries. I put the question, however, whether lords may take aids of this kind to maintain their own wars?

D. Surveys

65. FROM Hemming's cartulary, ed. T. Hearne, i. 287–8. The so-called Domesday *cartula* or record made before the Domesday commissioners concerning the liberty of Oswaldslow, 1086.

[*Heading*] *Indiculum* of the liberty of Oswaldslow Hundred confirmed upon oath by the whole county of Worcester in the reign of William I.

In the county of Worcester St. Mary of Worcester has a hundred called Oswaldslow, in which there are 300 hides whereof the bishop of that church, by ancient constitution, has all soke[1] and all customs therein as pertaining to the direct support of the church [*pertinentes ad dominicum victum*], together with both the king's service and his own, in such a way that neither the sheriff nor any other official exacting royal service can have any claim [*ullam querelam*] there, whether in pleas or anything else, and this by testimony of the county. And these 300 hides were of the demesne of that church, and in whatever way they might have been leased [*prestite*], and to whomsoever they might have been leased [*prestite*], in return for service to the bishop, he who held that leased land [*prestitam terram*] could in no way retain any custom to his own use except with the bishop's permission, nor could he retain the land beyond the term agreed between the parties, and in no circumstances could he go with the land [to another lord],[2] nor retain it by usurping hereditary right, nor could he claim it as his fee [*feudam suam*], except according to the will of the bishop and according to the agreement he had made with him. This testimony the whole county of Worcester confirmed by sworn oath on the initiative of the most holy and wise father in God, the lord bishop Wulfstan, in the time of king William I, before the magnates of the said king, that is to say Remigius, bishop of Lincoln, and earl Walter Giffard, and Henry de Ferrers, and Adam, brother of Eudo the king's dapifer, who had been sent by that same king to enquire into and set down in writing the possessions and customs both of the king and his magnates in this province and in many others, at the time when the said king caused all England to be surveyed. Hence in this matter, their inquest carried out and the witness of the entire county confirmed upon oath, they caused this testimony to be written down in an official royal document, henceforth to stand by royal authority, without challenge or dispute, and they adjudged the

[1] i.e. jurisdiction.
[2] Cf. the Domesday phraseology 'to go with his land to whatever lord he would', and the like, i.e. to place himself and the land under the lordship of another.

said liberty of the said hundred and the lands thereto pertaining to belong to the bishop in perpetuity, with the king's consent. In witness whereof a copy of it was, as I have said, written out in an official royal document, which is kept in the royal treasury with the surveys of all England.[3]

66. FROM the Worcestershire section of *Domesday Book* (London, 1783), i. 172*b*; Hemming's cartulary, as above, i. 72, 298–9. Translation only, *Victoria County Histories, Worcester*, i. (1901), 287–8.

Heading [from Hearne, i. 298] – The description of the land of the bishopric of the church of Worcester, according to the king's document [i.e. Domesday Book] which is in the royal treasury.[4]

The church of St. Mary of Worcester has one hundred, which is called Oswaldslow, in which there are 300 hides, whereof the bishop of that church, by ancient constitution, has all revenues from soke,[5] and all customs therein as pertaining to the direct support of the church [*pertinentes ad dominicum victum*], together with both the king's service and his own, in such a way that no sheriff can have any claim [*ullam . . . querelam*] there either in any plea or in any other matter whatsoever. This the whole county attests. These said 300 hides were of the demesne of the church and if any part of them were leased [*prestitum*] to any man[6] in return for service to the bishop, he who held that leased land could in no way retain any custom therefrom to his own use except with the bishop's permission, nor retain the land beyond the term agreed between the parties, and in no circumstances could he go with that land [to another lord].

67. FROM the Worcestershire section of *Domesday Book*, as above, i. 173*b*. Translation only, *Victoria County Histories, Worcester*, i. 294.

[Lands of the church of Worcester: hundred of Oswaldslow].
Of the same manor [*i.e.* Northwick] Urse[7] holds 5 hides at Hindlip and Alfreton[8] and Godfrey holds [them] of him. . . . Edric the steersman

---

[3] Cf. therefore Doc. 66 which is the official entry of this inquest in Domesday Book.
[4] Cf. No. 65 above.
[5] i.e. jurisdiction.
[6] Hemming improves upon this, by adding (e.g. p. 298) 'or allotted in any way'.
[7] Urse d'Abetot, the sheriff.
[8] Identified by Round as now Offerton Farm east of Hindlip.

K

held [them *i.e.* formerly] and performed his service with the other services pertaining to the king and the bishop.

68. FROM the Worcestershire section of *Domesday Book*, as above, i. 174. Translation only, *Victoria County Histories, Worcester*, i. 297.

To this manor [*i.e.* Phepson] belongs 1 berewick called Crowle. There are 5 hides that [pay] geld. Roger Laci holds [it], and Odo [holds it] of him. . . . Simund held it. It was [the church of Worcester's] demesne and he rendered for it to the bishop all service and geld and on no account could he go with that land [to another lord].

69. FROM the Worcestershire section of *Domesday Book*, as above, i. 172. Text and translation, C. W. Hollister, *Anglo-Saxon Military Institutions*, 66 and n.2: see also F. M. Stenton, *First Century of English Feudalism*, 118, n.1.

When the king goes on a military expedition, if anyone summoned by royal command remains behind, if he is so free a man that he has his soke and sake[9] and can go with his land to whom he pleases, he is in the king's mercy for all his land. If, however, the free man of some other lord stays away from the army, and his lord takes another man in his place, he [the absentee] shall pay 40 shillings to his lord who received the summons. But if nobody at all goes in his place, he shall still pay 40 shillings to his lord, but his lord shall pay the whole sum to the king.

70. FROM the Berkshire section of *Domesday Book*, as above, i. 56*b*. Printed, Stubbs, *Select Charters*, 107. Translation only, *English Historical Documents*, ii. 866.

If the king sent an army anywhere, only one soldier [*miles*] went from five hides and four shillings were given to him from each hide for his maintenance and wages for two months. This money, in fact, was not sent to the king but was given to the soldiers [*militibus*]. If anyone summoned on an expedition did not go, he forfeited all his land to the king. And if anyone having a reason for staying behind promised to send another in his place, and that substitute then failed to go, his lord was quit by the payment of fifty shillings.

71. FROM the Essex section of *Domesday Book*, as above, ii. 1. Translation only *Victoria County Histories, Essex*, i. 427–8.

[9] See p. 51 above.

The Essex section begins, as do all counties surveyed in Domesday, with a list of the holders of land (which serves therefore as a list of contents for what follows), the king and his tenants, the latter arranged in due order of precedence, ecclesiastics first. In this way the whole of the county was covered – i.e. *nulle terre sans seigneur.*

1. William King of the English.
2. The Holy Trinity of Canterbury.
3. The bishop of London.
4. The fief of the same bishop.
5. The canons of St. Paul.
6. The abbey of Westminster.
7. The bishop of Durham.
8. The canons of Waltham.
9. The abbey of Barking.
10. The abbey of Ely.
11. The abbey of St. Edmund.
12. The canons of St. Martin of London.
13. The abbey of Battle.
14. St. Valery.
15. The abbey of the Holy Trinity of Caen.
16. The abbey of St. Stephen of the same [i.e. Caen].
17. The abbey of St. Ouen [at Rouen].
18. The bishop of Bayeux.
19. The bishop of Hereford.
20. Count Eustace.
21. Count Alan.
22. W[illiam] de Warenne.
23. Richard son of count G[ilbert].
24. Swein of Essex.
25. Eudo the dapifer.
26. Roger de Otburville.
27. Hugh de Montfort.
28. Hamo the dapifer.
29. Henry de Ferrers.
30. Geoffrey de Magnaville.
31. The count of Eu.
32. Robert Gernon.
33. Ralph Baignard.
34. Ranulf Peverel.
35. Aubrey de Ver.
36. Peter de Valognes.
37. Ranulf, brother of Ilger.
38. Tihel the Breton.
39. Roger de Ramis.
40. John son of Waleran.
41. Robert son of Corbutio.
42. Walter the deacon.
43. Roger Bigod.
44. Robert Malet.
45. W[illiam] de Scohies.
46. Roger de Poitou.
47. Hugh de Gurnai.
48. W[illiam] Peverel.
49. Ralf de Limesy.
50. Robert de Toesni.
51. Ralf de Toesni.
52. Walter de Doai.
53. Matthew of Mortagne.
54. The countess of Aumale.
55. The countess Judith.
56. Frodo, brother of the abbot.
57. Saisselin.
58. Gilbert son of Turold.
59. William Levric.
60. Hugh de St. Quintin.
61. Edmund son of Algot.
62. Roger the marshal.
63. Adam son of Durand.
64. Goscelin le lorimer.
65. John nephew of Waleram.
66. William the deacon.
67. Walter the cook.
68. Moduin.
69. Ilbodo.
70. Haghebern.

71. Tedric Point[el].
72. Roger 'God save the ladies'.
73. G[ilbert] son of Salomon.
74. William son of Constantine.
75. Ansger the cook.
76. Robert son of Roscelin.
77. Ralf Pinel.
78. Robert son of Gobert.
79. Rainald the crossbow-
     man.
80. Gonduin.
81. Otto the goldsmith.
82. Gilbert the priest.
83. Grim.
84. Ulveva.
85. Edward.
86. Turchil.
87. Stanard.
88. Godwine.
89. Free men of the king.

72. FROM *The Red Book of Worcester* [late thirteenth century surviving in an eighteenth-century transcript], ed. M. Hollings, Worcestershire Historical Society, iv (1950), 412–13: collated[10] with *The Red Book of the Exchequer*, ed. H. Hall, (Rolls Series, London, 1896), i. 300–1, which is the official return of the bishop of Worcester to the feudal inquest of 1166, there headed 'Charter of the bishop of Worcester'.

The Knights of the Bishop.
These are those enfeoffed of the church.[11]
   The king 3 knights.
   The earl of Gloucester 7 knights and a half but he recognizes only one.
   Humphrey de Bohun 7 knights and a half but he recognizes only 4.
   William de Beauchamp 15 knights.
   Elias Giffard 1 knight.
   Henry de Novoforo 1 knight and he denies another.
   Gilbert de Minvers [*sic*][12] 1 knight, but he denies a fifth part.
   Walter de Clifford 1 knight.
   Hugh Poher 2 knights and a half.
   Hugh de Lacy 4 knights with William son of Herman who makes half a knight.
   Thomas de St. John de Plessy [*Placeto*][13] half a knight.
   Robert Marmion 2 knights but he denies one.
   John Marshal 1 knight and a half.
   Ralph Travers 4 parts of a knight.[14]
   These are those enfeoffed of old [*antiquitus*]
   Total 36 knights.[15]

[10] Only substantial differences are noted, and not e.g. minor variants of spelling.
[11] Presumably a general heading. In *R.B. Ex.* the first section is headed 'The Church of Worcester: these are those enfeoffed of old'.
[12] *R.B. Ex.* Mineriis.
[13] *R.B. Ex.* Aetrope Hasteng.
[14] i.e. four fifths. *R.B. Ex.* '1 knight less a fifth part'.
[15] *R.B. Ex.* 'This is the old enfeoffment. Total 37½ knights'.

These are those enfeoffed from the time of bishop Samson [1096–1112]

Adam de Crombe.[16] And this is the tenure of which he makes one knight: in Tidmington 3 hides; in Armescote 2 hides; in Earl's Croome 1 hide; in Blockley 1 hide [and 1] virgate. The following does not owe knight service [*non est de servitio militum*]: the said Adam established a title to 1 hide at Oddingley which was the land of a certain kinswoman of his, of the fee of the bishop but whereof the bishop had no service, and it is ancient tenure. The same [Adam] holds in Tredington one mill of the lord [bishop?] with 6 acres by [grant of] bishop Simon [1125–1150] which rendered in the time of king Henry I 29s. He also holds at Ripple: in Naunton half a hide of villein tenure which bishop Theulf [1115–23] lent [*acomodavit*] to Audam the glazier, which the aforesaid Adam bought from bishop Simon; and in addition to this many burgage tenures.

Frederic de Bissopesdone 1 knight[17] from the same period, and of this tenure there are 3 hides in Stratford and 2 hides in Fladbury.

Samson de Salcemarisco half a knight[17] from the same period and the tenure is: in Weston 4 hides, in Sudmede half a hide, in Brimesham 1 hide.

Illi de Turre 1 knight[18] from the same period and the tenure is: in Fladbury 2 hides and 1 virgate, in Grovehampton 1 hide, in Norton-by-Bredon 2 hides and 1 virgate, at Wick in Wichenford 1 virgate.

Jordan Destone half a knight[18] from the same period and the tenure is: in the tenure [*sic*] of Blockley 3 hides, but the third Roger Gulafre gave him with his sister in marriage, with a certain mill worth 5s. He also has there 1 virgate of land, which bishop Theulf leased to him for 4s. but Jordan withheld and withholds the rent, in addition to the assarts which he holds at Withington by [grant of] bishop Samson.[19]

These are those enfeoffed from the time of bishop Theulf[20] [1115–23].

Robert Devercy 1 knight.

Inge[21] 1 knight.

---

[16] R.B. Ex. Adam de Froile, where he is listed simply as owing 1 knight, without the details which follow in the Worcester text.

[17] The following details are not in R.B. Ex.

[18] The following details are not in R.B. Ex.

[19] R.B. Ex. has 'Total 4 knights' as an additional note to end this section.

[20] R.B. Ex. 'These are those enfeoffed from the demesne [*de dominico*] from the time of bishop Theulf'.

[21] Presumably the place, Ingon (in Hampton Lucy) Warwickshire, rather than a person. Cf. Book of Fees, 39. For 'Inge', R.B. Ex. has Thomas de St. John.

Bretone 1 knight.[22]
Huppeton, Oswin the Chamberlain half a knight.[23]
William de Edmundescote half a knight.
Prior of Worcester, half a knight.[24]

73. FROM *The Red Book of Worcester*, as above, iv. 432–4. 'Knight-service of the bishop of Worcester from the county of Worcester' [c.1164–79].

[i. The king's fee]
The lord king Henry son of Mathilda [*i.e.* Henry II] holds of the bishop of Worcester of the manor of Bredon in Bushley 1 hide subject to geld, and the earl of Gloucester [holds it] of the king. Also the lord king holds of the bishop of the manor in Queenhill 1 hide subject to geld which William de Kerdyf holds of him. Also the lord king holds of the bishop of the same manor in Barley 1 hide subject to geld and the earl of Gloucester of him. These above-written tenements the lord king holds of the bishop for two knights' fees [*per feodum duorum militum*]. Also the lord king holds in Gloucestershire of Bishop's Cleeve in Stoke Orchard[25] 5 hides and 1 virgate, and Archarius of him, for a knight's fee.
[ii]. The fees of William de Beauchamp.
William de Beauchamp holds of Roger bishop of Worcester [1164–79] ... [*the tenures and tenements are listed in terms of hides and virgates*] ...
And the sum total of all the hides which William holds of the bishop in the aforesaid 3 counties [of Worcester, Gloucester and Oxford] is 109½ hides. ...
... All these he says he holds of the bishop for a fee of 15 knights where there should be a fee of twenty-two knights at least except for half a hide.

74. FROM *The Red Book of Worcester*, as above, iv. 444–9: a list of knights' fees of the bishopric of Worcester, compiled 1208–9 for king John, subsequently copied out of the royal archives by the bishop's agent, Alfred de Northgrave, in 1298, and thereafter entered in the Red Book. The original return of 1208–9 is printed in *The Book of Fees*, (London, 1920) i. 35–9.

The bishop of Worcester owes to the lord king 49 knights and a half in

[22] *R.B. Ex.* 'Brotuere half a knight'.
[23] *R.B. Ex.* 'Peter de Uptune half a knight'.
[24] *R.B. Ex.* has 'Total 4 knights' as an additional note to end this section.
[25] Formerly Stoke Archer, from the family, and sergeanty, here referred to. Cf. *Book of Fees*, 39

all, that is to say in the counties of Worcester, Gloucester and Warwick. *Fees of the lord king.* Of which the lord king holds 4[26] fees, that is to say in Barley, in Bushley, Queenhill and in Broke [now Pull, in Bushley?]. *Knights of William de Beauchamp.* William de Beauchamp renders the said bishop service for 15 knights and a half[27] and denies ten fees.[28] The names and services are as under:

Richard de Walege 1 knight in Dorn [in Blockley] in the county of Worcester.

William son of Warin in Piddle and Moor [in Fladbury] one knight in the same county.

Roger de Lench' in Abbots Lench [in Fladbury] 1 knight and 2 hides in the same county.

Robert de Penedoke in Westmancote [in Bredon] 4 hides in the same county.

The same in Pendock 2 hides and a half in the same county.

Geoffrev de Apetot in Redmarley Dabitot 7 hides in the same county....

... Memorandum that 4 virgates of land make 1 hide, and five [four *written above in a later hand*] hides make 1 knight's fee.[29]

Total[30] of the knights' fees which the bishop holds of the king, 49 and a half.

Total of the knights' fees which the same king appropriated to himself from those fees, 26 knights' fees, and 46 hides which make nine knights' fees.

Total 25 fees [*sic* for 35?]

Knights of the bishop. [*Having thus dealt with the fees held of the bishopric by the king and by Beauchamp, the list then sets down the manors held by the bishop in demesne. In fact, much of this land is subinfeudated and, in those few cases where the appropriate details are given, the tenants of small parcels serve on the basis of five hides to a fee*] e.g.: (p. 445).

Northwick [in Claines]. The bishop holds in demesne the manor of Northwick in the county of Worcester, in which John Ruhere [*sic.* for Puher'?] holds of the bishop one knight in Churchill, Bredicot, Whittington and Spetchley....

... Ralph de Wylinter in Aston and Barbourne 1 hide by the service of a fifth part of one knight.

Richard Brihull' in Aston 1 hide by the service of a fifth part of one

[26] *Recte* 3. Cf. *Book of Fees*, 35; *Red Book of Worcester*, 412; *Red Book of the Exchequer*, 300; Doc. 72.

[27] *Book of Fees*, 35, 'for 15 knights'.

[28] *et decem feoda dedicit*, not in *Book of Fees*.

[29] This memorandum is not found in the *Book of Fees*, p. 36.

[30] The following notes of totals are not found in the *Book of Fees*.

knight. [*The list ends (p. 449) with the following note*][31]: Memorandum that the above-written fees were sought and found in the treasury of the Exchequer of the lord king at Westminster by Alfred de Northgrave in the month of May in the 26th year of the reign of king Edward son of king Henry. 1298.

[31] Not, of course, in the *Book of Fees*.

E. Artistic and Archaeological

75. FROM the Bayeux Tapestry (ed. F. M. Stenton and others, 2nd edition, London, 1965, Fig. 55). Norman knights at Hastings.

76. FROM the Bayeux Tapestry (as above, Fig. 51). The construction of Hastings castle.

77. Seals respectively of (a) Edward the Confessor (b) William the Conqueror.

78. Old Sarum, Wiltshire.

79. Pleshey, Essex.

75. Norman knights at Hastings, from the Bayeux Tapestry.

76. The construction of Hastings castle, from the Bayeux Tapestry.

77a.   Seal (both sides) of Edward the Confessor, from A. Wyon, *Great Seals of England*.

77b.   Seal (both sides) of William the Conqueror from A Wyon, *Great Seals of England*.

78. Old Sarum, Wiltshire (Crown Copyright – reproduced with permission of the Controller of Her Majesty's Stationery Office).

79. Pleshey, Essex (Reproduced with permission of the County Council of Essex).

INDEX

Figures relate to pages which may contain more than one reference to the subject listed.